The Process of Forgiveness

The Process
of
Forgiveness

WILLIAM A. MENINGER
O.C.S.O.

Continuum • New York

1997

The Continuum Publishing Company
370 Lexington Avenue
New York, NY 10017

Copyright © 1996 by William A Meninger

Printed in the United States of America

Library of Congress Catloging-in-Publication Data

Meninger , William.
The process of forgiveness / William A. Meninger.
      p.   cm.
   Includes bibliographical references.
  ISBN 0-8264-0888-5 (hbd.) 0-8264-1008-1 (pbk.)
   1. Forgiveness—Religious aspects—Christianity. I. Title.
BV4647.F55M46   1996
234'.5—dc 20   95-52494
                                              CIP

Preface from Mass of Reconciliation from *The Sacramentary.* (New York: Catholic Book Publishing Co., 1985).

All scriptural quotations are from the New International Bible.

The chapters on "Centering Meditation" and "Scriptural Meditation" are taken from the author's *1012 Monastery Road* (Petersham, Mass.: St. Bedes' Publications, 1989).

Quotes from *The Cloud of Unknowing and the Book of Privy Counseling* are from the William Johnston translation (New York: Doubleday/Image Books, 1973).

*This book is gratefully dedicated
to John and Helen Meninger,
Nick and Emily Cieri,
Jim and Carol Meninger,
Don and Joan Meninger,
John and Kay Santamaria,
and Vin and Pat Apruzzese
—lots of people
for lots or reasons.*

Father, all-powerful and ever-living God,
we praise and thank you through Jesus Christ our Lord
for your presence and action in the world.

In the midst of conflict and division,
we know it is you
who turn our minds to thoughts of peace.

Your Spirit changes our hearts:
enemies begin to speak to one another,
those who were estranged join hands in friendship,
and nations seek the way of peace together.

Your Spirit is at work
when understanding puts an end to strife,
when hatred is quenched by mercy,
and vengeance gives way to forgiveness.

For this we should never cease
to thank and praise you.

(From the Preface for Mass II of Reconciliation)

Contents

PART ONE—The Process

1   Five Stories of Forgiveness *11*
2   The Command to Forgive *16*
3   Why Forgive? *25*
4   Why Is Forgiveness So Difficult? *30*
5   What Forgiveness Is *34*
6   How and by Whom We Have Been Wounded *38*
7   What Do You Deserve? *45*
8   The Stages of Forgiveness *48*
9   The First Stage: Claiming the Hurt. *51*
10   The Second Stage: Guilt *56*
11   The Third Stage: Victim *59*
12   The Fourth Stage: Anger *63*
13   The Final Stage: Wholeness *68*

PART TWO—Nine Travelers

14   The Centers *75*
15   Mary, the Server *79*
16   Joe, the Winner *84*

17   Louise, the Romantic. *88*
18   Carl, the Thinker *92*
19   Ben, the Coordinator *96*
20   Peter, the Optimist. *99*
21   Esther, the Champion. *102*
22   Robert, the Pacifier *106*
23   Mildred, the Perfectionist *109*

PART THREE—Tools for Forgiveness

24   Scriptural Meditation *115*
25   Compassion Meditation ..... *121.*
26   Centering Meditation *126*
27   The Process of Focusing *138*
28   Vulnerability— An Ounce of Prevention *144*

Bibliography *151*

PART ONE

The Process

1
Five Stories of Forgiveness

Charles Reed was about to be released on parole. He had served eight years of a twelve-year sentence. Only thirty-three years old, he still had most of his life before him, but he had a past that he could never forget.

It all began when he was twenty-six, just two years out of college and already making his mark as a successful Denver real estate agent. A handsome man with an athletic appearance, he had spent his college years, as he put it, "catting around." With his well paying job, youthful energy, and good looks, he had become very much a man about town.

It was not unusual then for him to be seen one Saturday night escorting an attractive young lady to her apartment in a downtown Denver high-rise. Nor was it unusual either for him to be seen several hours later, leaving her apartment, going down to the parking lot, and driving away in his classy red sports car. What was unusual, however, was that the next morning when a friend tried to contact the young lady, she had to get the janitor to open her apartment door. She found her friend lying on her bed, hacked to death with a butcher knife.

Shortly afterwards, the police showed up at Charles's apartment. He was still sleeping and it took some effort to rouse him. A cursory search of his car, parked in his garage, revealed a bloody knife openly lying on the back seat.

It certainly seemed like an open-and-shut case. Charles, all the while protesting his innocence, was arrested, tried, found guilty, and given a twelve-year prison term. His parents sold their home and business in a futile effort to exonerate him, fully convinced by his protestations of innocence. Charles was a model prisoner and spent much of his time teaching inmates and learning the nonviolent approach to conflict resolution through Japanese martial arts.

After serving eight of his twelve years, and still maintaining his innocence, Charles was released on parole. It was at this point, through his case social worker (whom he later married) that I got to know him. After some time and several long conversations, I, too, became convinced that he was innocent and had been unjustly convicted and sentenced. Due to a legal technicality and some untempered zeal by state attorneys, certain evidence which should have led to the arrest of another person was not allowed to be presented in his trial. Charles is still working to have his conviction overthrown and his innocence legally established.

When I thought I knew him well enough, I asked him how he felt about it all. What was his reaction to the attorneys, the judge, the jury, the very legal system itself that destroyed not only his life but also the lives of his mother and father? He had a ready answer to my questions. Clearly he had given a great deal of weighty thought to these issues.

"For the first year," he said, "that I was in prison, I was bitter and angry and hated them all. Then I realized that I could no longer allow them to control my life, so I learned to love and forgive them."

My second story is also about a prisoner. Michael was eighteen years old, powerfully built and streetwise. He was hired by a wealthy, so-called business man as a bodyguard. It did not disturb him when he discovered that part of his duties consisted in helping to run drug-induced orgies, secretly videotaped and used to blackmail members of one of California's wealthier country clubs. What did bother Michael, however, was that when the racket was finally broken up by the police, he was arrested and convicted as responsible for the whole operation. His boss, by reason of wealth and political influence, was never even accused.

Michael was willing to admit his guilt but not willing to accept primary responsibility for the whole operation. So when the judge fixed the blame on him with an eight-year prison sentence, Michael was so enraged that he picked up a courtroom bench and attacked the judge. It took six policemen to restrain his fury. When things were under control, the judge changed the sentence to eight years in a prison for the criminally insane.

As he began his sentence, Michael's rage was unabated. He assaulted guards, threw his food against the wall and destroyed anything he could get his hands on. If he was not criminally insane when he was sentenced, he surely was now.

"It took me almost a year," he told me, "before I finally asked myself: just whom am I hurting?" I slowly began to realize that my rage had no effect at all on my former boss, the judge, or the legal system I was protesting. It was Michael and only Michael that I was attacking. Then I had to ask myself, how could I stop? It was not enough to cease my violent activity. The poison and the pain, the hatred and the anger, were hurting me so badly that I had to change from within. I was finally forced to realize that the only way I could escape from my real prison, the one I had built around myself, was to learn forgiveness and love. I did! It was not easy, but I have been free ever since."

My third story of forgiveness is similar and yet quite different. Sister Catherine, fifty-five years old, was the provincial superior of a large religious congregation of nuns. Medical diagnosis, after a series of dizzy spells, called for major brain surgery. It was performed successfully. In the recovery process, a tube was left inserted through an aperture in her skull for draining and antiseptic purposes. Two days after the operation, a shaken and distraught physician told her that he had been responsible for injecting into her brain a lethal solution. She would be dead in three hours!

At that time, Sister Catherine was alert and in full possession of all her faculties. She immediately called in her assistant provincial and the members of her provincial council. "There will be no repercussions," she declared. "No one is to be held at fault. There will be no medical claims or malpractice suits. I forgive without reservation anyone who may have been in any way responsible for what has happened." Two hours later she died.

My fourth story is about a group of people. As an organization, they call themselves MVFR— Murder Victims' Families for Reconciliation. Each person from this group has a personal story of his or her experience with the pain and wounds of having a loved one murdered— but also with the process of forgiveness and healing. They actually participate in organized tours reaching out to others by sharing their experiences. Most of them have moved painstakingly from their grief, denial, victimhood, and anger to survival and integral wholeness as they discovered the power of their own healing compassion to forgive the very murderers of their loved ones.

My last story, like the first two, is about a man who was the victim of legal injustice. Some have called him a political activist, but I do not think he would identify with that description. Perhaps he would more accurately be pictured as a social reformer. At any rate he was unjustly accused, illegally tried before a kind of "kangaroo court," and sentenced to death. The times were bad and the political situation uneasy, so his sentence had to be swiftly carried out. While his execution was being brutally accomplished, his friends abandoned him, and only his mother and a few of her friends remained at the scene.

When his physical pain and the psychological horror of his sufferings overwhelmed him, he cried out his despair and sense of abandonment. And then shortly before his bloody and shameful execution was finished, Jesus said, "Father, forgive them. They know not what they do," and he died.

These are captivating stories. They have an immediate and universal appeal. Why? What is there about forgiveness that strikes a sympathetic chord in our hearts? Why is it so significant and so important that even at the moment of death its healing power can make itself felt? We also must ask: If its fruits are so obvious, why is it so difficult? Why do some people nurture unforgiveness even for a lifetime? Why is it apparently even impossible for some people to forgive? Why do some people even say, "I want to forgive but I cannot?" Is this true? Is healing forever denied these people? I hope these questions will be answered in the following chapters as we pursue the process of forgiveness.

2

The Command to Forgive

Christianity is not the only religion to command forgiveness. It is at the heart of every significant religious, philosophical, ethical, psychological, or even political construct. The command to forgive is clear, universal, and as old as humanity. Gandhi, through his teachings on nonviolence, has been a strong witness to this. Christians are familiar, at least in theory, with the priority given to forgiveness. By the instructions of Jesus, it is an absolute necessity. Not only in theory and in his teachings has he insisted on it, but by his example as the final act of his earthly life.

Preachers are forever talking about forgiving enemies, turning the other cheek, walking the extra mile, and forgiving our brothers and sisters, not seven times, but seventy times seven times. One of the most powerful parables in the New Testament, that of the Prodigal Son, is about forgiveness. The Parable of the Lost Sheep also extols divine forgiveness. When teaching the Lord's Prayer, Jesus declares that forgiveness is one of the essential conditions out of which all our prayer must proceed if it is to be acceptable to the Father. St. Paul sums up the Christian command to forgive in his Letter to the Romans.

> Bless those who persecute you; bless and do not curse.
> Rejoice with those who rejoice; mourn with those who
> mourn. Live in harmony with one another. Do not be
> proud, but be willing to associate with people of low posi-
> tion. Do not be conceited.

> Do not repay anyone evil for evil. Be careful to do what is
> right in the eyes of everybody. If it is possible, as far as it
> depends on you, live at peace with everyone. Do not take
> revenge, my friends, but leave room for God's wrath, for it
> is written: "It is mine to avenge; I will repay." says the Lord.
> On the contrary: if your enemy is hungry, feed him; if he is
> thirsty, give him something to drink. (Ro 12:14–21)

Perhaps most significantly of all, Jesus insists that we cannot even approach God if we are not at peace with others. How
dramatic is the scene where he pictures a man or woman
approaching the altar with a gift to present to the Lord. "Therefore, if you are offering your gift at the altar and there remember that your sister or brother has something against you, leave
your gift there in front of the altar. First go and be reconciled to
your brother, then come and offer your gift (Mt 5:3–24)."

The command is clear, and how facilely we insist on it. If
you are to be a Christian, you must forgive! But how do we
forgive? What if we want to forgive but cannot? What if the
emotional trauma is so deep, the hurt so bad, the wounds and
scars so hideous, the offense so vivid that forgiveness is practi-
cally speaking beyond our power— or, at least, it seems to be.
What do we do as Christians, if we want to forgive, even if
only for our own sake, but cannot? Are we forever barred
from presenting our gift at the altar?

Seldom do we hear sermons on how to forgive. At times
we are even led to believe that forgiveness is simply an act of
the will. We make a decision to forgive, "to let bygones be
bygones," and the matter is settled. Sometimes we can do this;
more often we cannot.

We have all been hurt many times and probably have forgiven many times. Yet even when we think we have forgiven,

we often experience a sudden return of the humiliating rejection or abuse we have tried to forget. What do we do then as Christians? Can we bring our gift to the altar? What if the perpetrator of our hurts has died unforgiven? Are we forever barred from presenting our gift— a symbol of ourselves— to God?

Even when we think we have forgiven some hurt or offense, we often find that our wounds are still bleeding. Our lives are still affected. We are afraid to make new relationships; new challenges terrify us because of past experience of failures. We build walls around ourselves as protection to avoid a repetition of past injuries and to prevent people from getting close enough to hurt us again. Our life, or segments of it, is not a joy but a threat. Much of our time is spent in hiding from others and even from ourselves. We seek escape in dreams, drugs, imaginary illnesses, work, fantasy, food, sleep, or any of the many other escape routes modern society is so clever at presenting. We see ourselves sometimes, or all the time, as unbeautiful crippled creatures and project this unloving, low self-esteem on all our surroundings.

Do not these experiences lead us to believe that we have not really forgiven even when we have tried to? How then do we stand before God? What do we do when some past experience, recent or of many years standing, is so vivid and painful that we simply cannot forgive? Can we approach the altar and affirm our loving union with Christ in the holy sacrament of Communion? Can we honestly turn to our neighbor to give and receive the peace of Christ? Are we as hopeless, abandoned, and lost as we have sometimes felt ourselves to be? The Lord's Prayer sounds strong and clear—"Forgive us our trespasses as we forgive those who trespass against us."

So many of our problems arise, I think, from our misconceptions about forgiveness. We will look at these in some detail in subsequent chapters. Right now the most important thing for us to know is that forgiveness is usually not a simple act of the will. It is often a *process.* Sometimes the best we can do is merely to begin the process. The end of a journey is not its beginning. We must make the first step before we can make the last one. We all know that a journey of a thousand miles begins with one step and that it is better to light a single candle than to curse the darkness.

It would be much better if we could say: When you bring your gift to the altar, and then remember that your brother or sister has something against you, go and *begin the process of making peace* and then offer your gift. This helps us to grasp the two most important things we must realize if we are to forgive. It is a process, not a once-and-for-all act of the will and we *need* to present ourselves at the altar, that is, we need God's help.

The most authentic sign we can give ourselves that we have actually begun the process of forgiveness is our prayer. This is true even if the only prayer we can say is to ask to want to forgive. In the beginning it may be too much for us even to pray for the person who hurt us. Perhaps all we can do is to pray for ourselves—to pray that for our own sake we may begin the process of forgiveness. This can be the first step in our journey.

Let me tell you the story of Stephanie. Stephanie was a very sad woman. She was forty-seven years old, unhappily married, with three grown children and low self-esteem. She told me that nothing she ever did was worthwhile because she herself was not worthwhile, and from nothing, nothing comes. Tracing the source of her misery to a horror that happened thirty-two years ago when she was fifteen, Stephanie identified herself with that incident which had become the focal point of her life. She had been gang-raped by five teenage boys. All younger than her, they got off with minimal punishment and went on with their lives. Stephanie's was destroyed.

She identified herself as a victim. She was violated, impure, and unclean—although completely innocent of any provocation, she kept reliving the attack to see how she might have been in some way responsible. Her whole life was colored by her self-loathing, rejection, and low self-esteem. For a few years she had even become a prostitute, feeling it was the only suitable profession left for her.

Her feeling for the five boys was a constant, intense loathing and repulsion. Wherever they were, she felt they were living their lives freely, unhindered by what they had done, without even a legal record of their crime. Meanwhile, her own life was in shambles. She felt that they were still violating her and making her a despicable object of contempt.

She had finally reached the point where she had to do something or her past would destroy even her very hold on life itself. To talk about her experience was very difficult. No one, not even her husband, knew of her background. Humiliated and ashamed by what had happened to her and by the way she had reacted to it all her adult life, she could not speak of it without giving way to a paroxysm of grief and tears.

"I know," she said, "that I have to forgive them. But my memory of what they did and the lifelong misery they are responsible for makes my hatred for them stronger and forgiveness impossible. I cannot bring myself to receive Holy Communion. When I give the kiss of peace at Mass, I realize it is sheer hypocrisy, so I have stopped going to church altogether. I realize I am condemning myself at this point, but what can I do?"

Stephanie did not realize it, but the simple fact of her asking that question, "What can I do?" and coming to talk about it was for her the first step of a long journey. She had begun. The movement was initiated, and she was going forward.

My first suggestion was for her to pray for herself, to pray that God would lead her to forgiveness. This she could do even though it was too soon for her to attempt to pray for her perpetrators. Then I prayed with her and for her. I also briefly and cautiously included those five boys in my prayer. Without actually realizing it, she was able to say "Amen." She was surprised and even pleased when I called this to her attention.

No longer did she have to leave her gift at the altar. It was indeed more important than ever for her to approach the Lord for help and grace through the sacraments. Stephanie still had a long way to go, but she had begun. Two weeks later she even told me that she was finally able to add on to her own prayers for God's help, a request that God would deal mercifully with those boys. She did not feel that she could yet forgive them but realized that the process of healing had begun and no longer wished them harm.

God's place in the process of forgiveness is especially important. Prayer is simply a way of acknowledging this. It is a reassuring turn to God when what we must do seems to be unlikely or too difficult or even impossible. It is a giant first step, one that is pregnant with hope, faith, and eventually, as we will experience, love. In love will be found forgiveness.

It is good for us to be aware of God's role in every step of the forgiveness process. It is especially important in the beginning of that process. We could not begin without God's grace, and we often have begun, i.e., received God's grace, without even realizing it. I have given many workshops on forgiveness. Most of the participants are there because they find forgiveness very difficult, even impossible. One of the first things that I do is to reassure them that they have already received and responded to God's help. Otherwise they would not even be present at the workshop. I now say the same to anyone who has gotten this far in reading this book!

In Mt 5:43, Jesus tells us:"You have heard that it was said, 'Love your neighbors and hate your enemy'. But I tell you: Love your enemies and pray for those who persecute you." And in Lk 11:13 he says: "If you then, though you are evil, know how to give good gifts to your children, how much more will your Father in heaven give the Holy Spirit to those who ask him!" These two statements are closely related. The Holy Spirit whom the Father will send to us is the spirit of love and reconciliation. So if we feel we can't forgive our enemies, all we have to do is to call upon God in prayer for his Holy Spirit. Forgiveness will proceed then, not from us, but from the Spirit of God.

Prayer does many things for us in the area of forgiveness. Sometimes we may not even be aware of them but its effects are powerful. As we have already said, prayer can be the beginning of the journey towards forgiveness of others and towards self-healing. It is a way of recognizing and acknowledging God's movement towards us and God's gift of grace.

This grace often involves an element of surprise. The Spirit blows where the Spirit wills. No one knows whence the Spirit comes or where the Spirit goes. Where the Spirit is present, we experience God's power. It is always something more than we ever realize we can do and the fruits of the Spirit working in us accomplish results we could never expect, plan on, or foretell. Prayer is a manifestation of the Spirit's presence in our lives.

The unexpectedness of the Spirit's grace and its power is like standing before an impenetrable wall—too high to climb, and too long to walk around. We stand before a solidly sealed door without a knob, a bell, or any means of opening. To be free, we must pass through that door. We simply stand there (a symbol of prayer) and, suddenly, the door opens wide spontaneously from the other side! "Knock and the door will be opened to you" (Mt 7:7).

Pray in any way that you can. Read the Psalms, use a prayer book, say the rosary. Maybe this will be the best you can do for starters. But pray for healing, for the power to forgive. At some point you should try to pray in your own words. Bring your hurts, your sorrows, your heartbreaks, your loneliness to the Lord. If this is what you have, this must be the gift you bring to the altar. At times this gift may be only your confusion, your despair, even your anger. Prayer avoids denial and brings you to face real issues. Things you may never be able to say to another human being, you can bring to the Lord who already knows them, In parts II and III of this book, I will share some specific kinds of prayer and indicate certain types of personalities that might profit from them.

God wants this from you because you need it. You need the opportunity to express your frustration, your sorrow, your sense of injustice, or your rage. When you pray, coming from any of these feelings, you know that you have begun. The Lord will take your hand and accompany you on the journey ahead. There will be surprises in store. We will begin to see our responsibilities, our part in the forgiveness process. Perhaps God will enlighten us regarding those who have wounded us. Maybe God will bring us to a realization that they too are his children and also carry hurts.

Prayer gives us access to God's love. It is communication and openness to God and to God's love. Without this communication nothing can happen "for He Himself is our peace who has made the two one, and has destroyed the barrier, the dividing wall of hostility . . ." (Eph 2:14). We have been given the message of reconciliation. Prayer is the way to receive it. "Therefore, if anyone is in Christ, he is a new creation: the old has gone, the new has come! All this is from God, who reconciled us to Godself through Christ and gave us the ministry of reconciliation" (2Co 5:17–18).

Let me suggest two scripture texts that you might read, pray over, and enter into for meditation. Read the Parable of the Prodigal Son in Lk 15:11–32. Be the father. Go through his experience of having his younger son ask for his inheritance and then leave home with it. Experience the feelings of the father, his concern, his loss, and then his forgiveness and joy at his son's return. Then be the older brother. See the justice of his complaint. Question it even as the father does. What effect do the words of the father have: "But we had to celebrate and be glad, because this brother of yours was dead and is alive again; he was lost and is found." (Lk 15:32)

Finally be the younger son. Feel his cruelty to his father, his disdain for what his home had to offer. See and experience his downfall, his loss of fortune, his hunger, and then his hope at the thought of returning to his father's house. Know the joy he felt at his father's forgiveness. Let God speak to you and to your issues through this parable.

Next read the story of the blind man, Bartimaeus, at the gates of Jericho (Mk 10:46). Be that man. Experience his blindness, his helplessness. Hear the approach of Jesus, and cry out to him. Continue to cry out even in the face of discouragement. Hear Jesus call you to come to him, and hear him ask you what you want him to do for you. Answer him!

3

Why Forgive?

Should we forgive simply because it is commanded? Did God arbitrarily decide one day that forgiveness would be a good thing and so make it obligatory? Certainly not. Forgiveness is demanded by the very nature of man and woman. It is not only divine, it is also human. God commands it because without it we are less than human, with it we are more. Forgiveness is a human need, and there are many reasons for it.

One of the classic scripture texts already quoted in part is Mt 5: 44–48:

> . . . love your enemies and pray for those who persecute you, that you may be [children] of your Father in heaven. He causes the sun to rise on the evil and the good, and sends rain on the righteous and the unrighteous. If you love those who love you, what reward will you get? Are not even the tax collectors doing that? And if you greet only your brothers [and sisters], what are you doing more than others? Do not even pagans do that? Be perfect, therefore, as your heavenly Father is perfect!

This can be a troublesome text indeed. Be perfect as God is perfect! Isn't Jesus demanding the impossible? Not really. A close look at the text will help us to understand what Jesus means by being perfect as the Father is perfect. He causes the sun to shine and the rain to fall on everyone without partiality

or distinction. The Father loves all his children without conditions, and we are told to love one another the same way.
Indeed if we are to love one another for the love of God, it
must also be that very love of God which we have for each
other. This is an unconditional love. We love our families and
our enemies—those who support us and those who have
hurt us. But why?

Love of God is the Great Commandment. It must be
attempted with the totality of our being—our whole heart and
soul, mind and body. Insofar as is possible in this life, it must be
unconditional. We cannot say, "I would love God if . . . " or "I
will love God when . . . " These are conditions. Likewise with
others. We must attempt to love them also unconditionally.
Thus we cannot say, "I would love her if only she . . . ," "I could
love them if they would . . . ," or "I will love him when he . . . "

Now we are getting closer to understanding why we must
forgive. It is the only way to love as God loves, i.e., unconditionally. But there is something more we must understand.
This "something more" is crucial and once we understand it,
we will make giant strides in our process of forgiving. We
must love *ourselves* unconditionally! In fact this must be the
model and the motive for our love of others. "Love your
neighbor as yourselves." How can we do this if we hate ourselves, have low self-esteem, identify ourselves as victims—
the fruit of hurt, rejection, or abuse.

It is extremely important from the very beginning to
understand that the primary consideration and motivation for
forgiveness is ourselves. We forgive others, in the first place,
for our own sake. This is why God commands it of us. This is
why it is a human need. It is only when we forgive that we are
free. Recall the stories of Charles Reed and Michael. They
were prisoners sentenced to jail terms, but both of them realized that the real prisons that held them were of their own
making. Hatred, rage, anger, and vengeance were simply four
more prison walls, ones they built around themselves, and

they dedicated all of their energy to strengthening them. They used these passions to rub salt into their wounds to prevent them from healing. It was only when they decided to stop hurting themselves, to permit the wound to heal and allow forgiveness to happen, that they were freed from their real, self-inflicted prisons.

IN THE SCRIPTURES, God speaks to us in a human language and in the human manner. Sometimes it sounds like God is putting conditions on love. Look at the Our Father. "Forgive us our trespassers as we forgive those who trespass against us." Is this not a condition? It is, but notice: it is a condition which we place on ourselves. God does not condemn us, we condemn ourselves.

Jesus uses a very human language to express himself. Sometimes it does sound vengeful, hateful, and condemnatory, i.e., conditional. Look at the Parable of the Wicked Servant. (Mt 18:32–34). When he refused to forgive the debt of someone else as the master had forgiven his debt, the master said:

> "You wicked servant. . . . I cancelled all that debt of yours because you begged me to. Shouldn't you have had mercy on your fellow servant just as I had on you?" In anger his master turned him over to the jailors to be tortured until he should pay back all he owed
>
> This is how my heavenly Father will treat each of you unless your forgive your brother from your heart.

This threat must be seen in the full context of God's unconditional love, in the total giving of his Son who died for our sins and rose for our justification. In fact, it isn't God who tortures us but we who torture ourselves. Only when we allow our wounds to heal and let forgiveness occur will we free ourselves from our self-imposed prison cells. We forgive them for our own sakes. Forgiveness is for us.

A very important reason, then, to forgive is our own happiness. Isn't it strange that the very reason we hold on to unforgiveness is that, in some perverted way, we convince our-selves that not forgiving will contribute to our happiness. We must see that it won't. We must see that our negativity, our deficiencies, our weaknesses, and our low self-esteem all come from a long series of wounds and hurts that we have experienced and out of which we are acting (or hiding). The actions of a broken person will be broken acts. The life of a victim will be itself victimized. When we allow ourselves to remain wounded, bitter, resentful persons, we contaminate not only ourselves but everyone we contact. Our family, our children, our friends, our community, our society, our very world is marred, soiled, and degraded. We shrivel our own capacity to love and be loved, to trust and be trusted, and affect also the abilities of those around us to love and to trust. When I do not forgive someone who has injured me, I simply continue that evil and allow it to affect the well-being of everyone else.

Dr. Sidney Simon calls the perpetuating of the cycle of abuse the ultimate dead-end street (see bibliography). Repeat-edly we do unto others as they have done unto us. Repeated patterns of abused children becoming abusive parents are well documented. Children who have been abused verbally, physi-cally, or sexually will be triggered to unleash the same patterns of violence on their own children. We even set ourselves up for repeated patterns of abuse, violence, rejection, or ridicule according to the responses we learned as children, and, then, pass these horrors on to our own children. Fortunately we can break the cycle and free both ourselves and our dependents from this dead-end street.

There are, of course, many seemingly powerful and com-pelling reasons not to forgive. But hasn't the whole world suf-fered for decades under the "reasonable" threat by "reasonable" people of nuclear annihilation, of tobacco-induced lingering illnesses, and from the "reasonable" ingestion of alcohol and other drugs. Human reason does not always provide the answers. This is why we need the revelation of God in the

Church and the Scriptures and, ultimately, the commandment there to forgive.

One of my favorite comic strips is Calvin and Hobbes. In one of them, Calvin, a six-year-old, asks his father, "Dad, how does a bunch of soldiers killing one another solve the world's problems?" His father, at a loss for words, just stares at Calvin with a pained expression on his face. Calvin shrugs and walks away saying, "I think that grown-ups just *act* like they know what they are doing." Another cartoon character, Pogo the 'Possum, is fond of saying, "We have met the enemy and he is us."

There are many logical illusions that we cherish which support our refusal to forgive. These are put forth by our false-self systems so that we may pursue what erroneously seems to be the easiest path, i.e., staying in our self-built prisons. We claim sometimes that by not forgiving we protect ourselves from being hurt again. By rubbing salt in our wounds, we keep our guard up lest others repeat their rejection, abuse, deception, or betrayal. And what a price we pay! Not forgiving also can give us the deceptive feeling that we are maintaining power over those who hurt us—especially if we were hurt as children. We can hate them, and there is nothing they can do about it. How much more power would we have if we could love them. Not forgiving also allows us to escape the responsibility that comes from freedom. Forgiveness means that you can no longer blame someone else for the course your life takes. You alone are responsible. How much easier it is to have an evil perpetrator to blame for everything that goes wrong.

4
Why Is Forgiveness So Difficult?

If forgiveness is so important and so necessary for Christian commitment, human wholeness, and personal and communal happiness, why is it so difficult? Much of the answer lies in our misunderstandings regarding forgiveness. These stem not from what forgiveness is but from what forgiveness is not. Many of the problems that stand in the way of our extending personal forgiveness to those who have hurt us will simply disappear once we understand what forgiveness is not.[1]

Forgiveness is not forgetting. The admonition to "forgive and forget" is often not possible. Indeed true forgiveness is just the opposite. It is mindfulness—an awareness of what has happened and of its true value in your life. At times we refuse to forgive because we think that this means we have to bury some past painful event or at least pretend that it never happened. Forgiveness is not forgetting. We remember the pain and will always bear the scar of a past hurt. To forget injuries can mean that we are passing by a learning experience. Past hurts can actually be gifts in disguise. Forgetting may be

---

[1] For a more extensive treatement of this subject, see Sidney Simon and Suzanne Simon, *Forgiveness* (New York: Time Warner Books, 1991), 14–24.

possible when wounds are healed and forgiveness has occurred, but it is a by-product of forgiveness and not a necessary one. Forgetfulness is possible but only in the sense that the pain that once controlled and ruled over us does so no longer. The memory may well be permanent.

It is unhealthy and unrealistic to try to forget or minimize hurts just as it is unhealthy and unrealistic to brood over them or exaggerate them. We learn from the past. Experience shows us that remembering helps us to grow, enables us to redirect our energies, and contributes toward the breaking of the cycle of abuse. It is no wonder then that people often turn from forgiveness when they confuse it with forgetfulness. We hear people say, "I can never forgive her for what she did to me." Usually by this they mean, "I can never forget what she did to me," or, at the least, they confuse the two even in their own minds . It can, indeed, be very helpful for us to understand that the two attitudes are not at all the same.

Neither does to forgive mean to condone. When someone hurts us, they have hurt us. It is painful and has an effect on our life. To forgive the perpetrator of harm is not to say that what he/she did was all right or even to try to minimize it.

Neither is forgiveness a form of absolution. When we forgive, we are not letting someone off the hook. They must still answer for what they have done, to you, to society. to themselves, to God. This is up to them, not up to you. Yes, to forgive is divine. It does share in the unconditional love which comes from God—but only God gives absolution—and only the sinner can seek it. Even when we forgive the harm another has done to us, we are not, by that very fact, either condoning or absolving the guilt or the responsibility of the perpetrator. It is certainly true that some people do not deserve to be forgiven: active child abusers, mass murderers, spouse beaters, dope peddlers—the list is endless. Especially when they themselves are not seeking forgiveness. We don't forgive for their sake but for our own. Otherwise, we waste our energy which should be used for getting on with our own lives. We are the ones who must pay a price for unforgiveness, not the perpetrators.

Rabbi Joseph Gelberman, whose entire family was exterminated in the Nazi Holocaust, states he has forgiven because he had to let go of what happened. Many of his Jewish colleagues who survived the Holocaust brought Hitler with them to America and still carry all the horrors of the concentration camps about with them. He reminds them of the farewell address of Moses to the Israelites: "This day I call heaven and earth as witnesses against you that I have set before you life and death, blessings and curses. Now choose life, so that you and your children may live" (Dt 30:19). When we chose healing, wholeness, and forgiveness, we choose blessings and life.

Forgiveness is not a pretense. It is not a heroic acceptance of a past hurt which simply must be borne so that life can go on. We cannot brush off our crosses and their wounds by attributing them to the "will of God" and thus grinning and bearing them. The will of God in such events is found in what we make of them. True forgiveness does not come from a super effort of the will which must be put forth if we are to be Christians. When forgiveness comes, it is more like something that happens to us than something we make a great effort to do. It comes, as it were, as a by-product of our healing. When our wounds are healed, our hurts comforted, and our self-esteem restored, we will discover that there are no reasons to hold back forgiveness. It happens almost of its own accord spontaneously, openly, and freely. It does not require great self-sacrifice or martyrdom.

Forgiveness is not a once-and-for-all decision. Even when it has taken place freely and spontaneously, the hurts it involves can be triggered by present events although time and healing will diminish that happening more and more. We must remember that it is not only an act of the will, something we decide to do, but has many feeling and emotional levels. The memory of past suffering will always be there, but it does not have to be painful. It cannot be willed away.

The freedom which comes with forgiveness brings new responsibilities which require new decisions. When we forgive someone, we say, "You are no longer to be allowed to govern my life. Henceforth I will be responsible for what I do—not as reactions to your infliction but from my own free decisions. I have set myself free, and I will live my life as I choose it."

Forgiveness is not a sign of weakness but of strength. We do not need our anger to protect ourselves. Our strength will come from our love and our freedom. Our forgiveness is not dependent on who the perpetrator was, what he or she did to me, whether or not they will do it again, or even if they think they are getting off scot-free. It is not primarily for them that I forgive but for myself.

It is not unusual for someone to so identify with their wounds that they become all victim. This becomes their self-identity. For them to forgive means to lose their identity. This indeed is true, but the identity they lose is their false self. Their specialness changes. It is not taken away. Do we really want to be special by the way we bleed over ourselves and over others?

Forgiveness does not entail a loss of face or a weakness. Remember the stories with which we began this book—five people who forgave and who are admired for their integrity and strength. Unforgiveness at times gives us the illusion that we have some kind of a hold on our offenders or that we are, in this way, able to keep them indebted to us—even when the injurer does not acknowledge such debts.

Forgiveness, then, is not forgetting. It is not condoning or absolving. Neither is it pretending nor something done for the sake of the offender. It is not a thing we just do by a brutal act of the will. It does not entail a loss of identity, of specialness, or of face. It does not release the offenders from obligations they may or may not recognize. An understanding of these things will go a long way towards helping people enter into the forgiveness process. Having seen what forgiveness is not, in the next chapter we will consider what forgiveness really is.

5

What Forgiveness Is

Forgiveness is a form of realism. It allows us, perhaps for the first time in our life, to see ourselves, others, and events of our life as they really are. It does not deny, ignore, minimize, camouflage, or excuse what others have done to us or how we have suffered from their acts. When we forgive, we enable ourselves to look squarely at our wounds and their scars. We can see how much energy we have wasted by not forgiving, and we begin to realize how much we have going for ourselves as we move on with our lives.

Forgiveness means we no longer want to take revenge on our offenders. Often this is impossible anyway, but now the energy expended on evening the score is freed for better things, for more positive ways of enhancing our own lives. We realize that we can never really get even. To take an eye for an eye does not return our own loss. Forgiveness allows us to accept the inner peace that comes when we allow ourselves to stop our frustrating efforts at punishing offenders. Gandhi says somewhere that if we all lived by "an eye for an eye" the whole world would be blind!

Forgiveness allows us to realize that we are more than victims of abuse and injustice. We don't need our hatreds, resentments, and brooding over wrongs. We acknowledge that these things are valueless both as weapons to punish others or as defenses to keep people far enough away from us so that they will not be able to hurt us again.

Forgiveness gives us both a power and a freedom over ourselves and over others:

> You have heard that it was said: "Eye for eye, and tooth for tooth." But I tell you. Do not resist an evil person. If someone strikes you on the right cheek, turn to him the other also. And if someone wants to sue you and take your tunic, let him have your cloak as well. If someone forces you to go one mile, go with him two miles (Mt 5:38–42).

I really do not think that Jesus is here issuing a command but rather describing a reality. When we forgive, which is really what he is talking about here, we are able to do these things. We are empowered to do them freely, nonviolently, and without losing our personal integrity. They become a means, in the best sense of "heaping coals on our enemy."

Consider, for a moment, the sentence of Jesus, "If someone forces you to go one mile, go with him two miles." Palestine in Jesus' time was under the military domination of the Roman Empire and was occupied by the Roman Army. The military law permitted a Roman soldier to order a civilian to carry his equipment for up to one mile. Jesus is saying that a truly free (i.e., forgiving and nonviolent) person will be able not only to carry the equipment for the required mile, but he will be so little affected or constrained by the law and the soldier's command that he will be able and willing (i.e., be free) to go an extra mile. Who is really empowered in such a situation, the soldier or the civilian? Going the extra mile, giving the cloak, turning the other cheek is not an expression of either masochism or penance, but of power and true freedom.

Forgiveness is the decision that we have done enough futile hiding, suffering, hating, and fantasizing revenge. It is an awareness that the things we have done to ourselves do not affect our offenders, and that we are through hurting ourselves. We are going to stop being the child who "goes out to eat worms" to get back at her parents.

Forgiveness is true freedom. It releases us from being stuck to a cruel event of our past which had stopped the progress of our lives and oriented us to pain and regret. We become free to pursue a better way to real growth and maturity—to become what we should be rather than remain an underdeveloped, frightened child glued to the horror of a past abuse.

Forgiveness frees our life. It becomes full of surprises, and we recognize that "little bit of good news" that awaits proclamation in each one of us, as the philosopher Unamuno reminds us. A brand new life awaits us once we opt for forgiveness and the freedoms it bestows. Our injuries, wounds, and scars bring forth a wonderful and unexpected gift, the freedom to start anew. As the Book of Sirach puts it:

> A joyful heart is life itself, and rejoicing lengthens one's life span. Indulge yourself and take comfort and remove sorrow from you, for sorrow has destroyed many and no advantage ever comes from it. Jealousy and anger shorten life and bring on premature old age (Sir 30:22–24).

Forgiveness recognizes that wounds can heal and that scars which are always left behind can become even stronger than the original unwounded tissue.

In the very dramatic ceremony that begins the celebration of Christ's Resurrection, the Easter Vigil, the wounds of Christ are marked by the insertion of five grains of incense on the paschal candle. The priest then proclaims them to be "resplendent and glorious." Forgiveness allows us to unite our wounds to those of Christ. We are free to allow our sufferings to be redemptive and to "fill up in my flesh what is still lacking in regard to Christ's afflictions" (Col 1:24). I remember a conversation I had some twenty years ago with a friend who was a Baptist preacher. "How terrible it is," he lamented, "not that there is so much suffering in the world but that it is wasted—when it could be redemptive even as were the sufferings of Our Savior."

Forgiveness allows us to respect our injurers, to allow them to be responsible for what they have done. At the same time, it frees us from letting their offenses loom so large that our injuries define who they are. Just as we are more than a victim, so our offenders are more than the bestowers of injuries. Only forgiveness and the freedom and love which it releases can lead us to this understanding and compassion.

Forgiveness is a releasing of all the negative emotions connected with past incidents. It allows us to let go of the strange and harmful reactions that past injuries trigger in our lives and which lead to the cycle of repetitive abuses.

Forgiveness is a sign and cause of a positive self-esteem. It is more than a response to the Christian command to love as an ethical imperative or a moral obligation. It stems from and further enhances this positive self-esteem. It allows us to love ourselves not because we are ordered by God to do so but because we recognize the inherent value and self-worth that God has given us. Simply put, we are worth loving and we know it.

Finally, forgiveness is a process. We have already said that it is not a cold, disembodied act of the will whereby we grit our teeth and do it. It takes time. Rather, the healing takes time and forgiveness results from the healing. Forgiveness is not something we do directly but is something that happens to us. When we stop rubbing salt in our wounds and do whatever is required for it, our wounds will heal. When we allow this healing to take place, we will discover that forgiveness has also taken place. There will be nothing left to forgive or to hold back.

In the forgiveness process there are recognizable stages which we go through and which have been carefully studied and documented. While these stages are not as distinct and clear as we make them out to be in teaching and describing them, they are discernable. Knowing what they are facilitates their progress and enables us to move on more confidently in the process. We will soon discuss these stages and examine what is needed to get the most out of each one as we pass through them. First, however, we would do well to consider ways in which we have been hurt and who has hurt us.

6

How and by Whom We Have Been Wounded

It is with a certain hesitancy that I raise the questions about ways we have been hurt and by whom the hurts have been inflicted. There is controversy today concerning psychological counselors who are supposedly resurrecting long-buried memories of sexual abuse during infancy and early childhood. Stories are becoming more and more frequent concerning devil cults and witchcraft practices involving sexual molestation of children, the memories of which are then buried in their subconscious by repression, by some spell, or by some form of hypnotism. Some counselors claim that these early experiences, even though forgotten, poke through into our consciousness by triggering certain abnormal reactions, emotions, and fears. There are lists of as many as thirty-five abnormal reactions to be discerned in adults who have been the victims of such treatment. In the past two years I have had to deal with five women with such experiences. All of them claimed to have forgotten the abuse until their memories were triggered either by hypnotism or by reading about others who were subject to cruel treatment.

I am not comfortable with every instance of dredging up past traumatic events that our subconscious has buried. I do not think that this kind of "forgetfulness" is always unhealthy. There seems to be a natural tendency of the human psyche to act this way in order to protect the growing child from the horrors of their experiences. In a given case when the memories are brought to light, we can make a judgment as to whether it was helpful or not to a particular person. Beforehand, however, I have some doubts as to whether we should stir up calm waters (if they are really calm waters, of course).

With this reservation, then, I would now like to raise the question regarding ways in which we have been hurt. All of us certainly have been wounded at some time or other. The ways are myriad. Disappointment is one way. We have all been disappointed but sometimes it takes on traumatic overtones with a lasting impact. It can hurt with a feeling closely related to despair. This is particularly so when the disappointment is coupled with an injustice. Not to get a promotion we expected and deserved can be life-shattering. Disappointments for a child can be especially traumatic and in areas that significant adults often do not realize. I recall one woman of thirty-five speaking of her disappointment when her father failed to show up at her first birthday party at seven years— and of the guilt she had to deal with when she learned that his absence was caused by an automobile accident which almost killed him. Disappointment may have little to do with responsibility or bad intentions. It simply happens, and it hurts.

Another way in which we can be hurt is rejection and its close relation, betrayal. I am even today in awe of the pain I suffered at six years old when my two best friends decided to "gang up" on me. We had made a blood pact of friendship and, for some unknown reason, they thought it would be amusing to turn on me. It did not last long, and we were soon friends again, but the memory and the reaction it later triggered endured for years. The message that rejection sends to us, whether temporary or permanent, is that we are not good enough. The wounds of being rejected can scar us to the point where our self-esteem is seriously shot. Robert, at forty-five years of age, has still to forgive his father for years of rejection in favor of his older brother who was an athletic wonder. Robert is greatly talented in other areas, but his whole life has been tainted by an attitude that nothing he does is ever good enough. His father, who is now dead, never realized how he had rejected Robert.

Abandonment is a very common way of receiving hurts. The death of a parent is often perceived by a very young child as abandonment, and it may take years before the child brings himself to forgive this—it may even take years before the child actually realizes that forgiveness is necessary. Abandonment through divorce or adoption also wreaks its havoc. The breaking of any strong emotional bond between ourselves and a significant other is terribly painful no matter how justified the cause and how innocent the perpetrator. We can spend years running from the involvement of further bonds that have the potential for leading to abandonment.

We are often hurt by ridicule and humiliation. Children especially are prone to provoke these hurts and to receive them. Anything out of the ordinary, from wearing glasses, obesity, acne, ethnic background, and so forth, can be used to ridicule or humiliate. I remember in my years as an undergraduate, I was in a situation where any sort of scholarly excellence was reacted to by peers with ridicule. It was a matter of humiliation to do anything in the academic arena that would mark you off as "a brain." Frustration and bitterness result from such hurts that can last for years.

Humiliation can take many strange forms. Maria recalls being present before her father's coffin when she was six years old. She does not remember crying but she must have done so because some adult—again, she does not remember who— mistakenly tried to "help her." This woman bent over in front of her and said, "Now you don't want to cry, dear. Do you think your father would want this? Let me see you smile!" The bitterness is still in Maria's voice as she recounts how this woman, thinking she was being helpful, actually forced her to smile before her father's dead body. Not even remembering who she was, Maria is working on forgiving her forty years later.

Deception is yet another cause of deep hurts. Sometimes deceptions last for years and become a way of life, actually known to all, but never openly acknowledged. Jeff's father was in jail serving a life sentence for murder. His mother, "for Jeff's sake," had moved to a new neighborhood, got a new job, and ceased any communication with her husband's only living relative, a brother. She would never permit Jeff to mention his father and never spoke of him. She had to know that Jeff was old enough to read the papers during his father's celebrated trial and conviction, but they both maintained, even with each other, a deceptive pretense. Today, Jeff has more trouble trying to forgive his mother than his father, whom he visits regularly.

When adults lie to a child, the child attempts to come up with his or her own answers. Usually such answers are somehow directed against the child. The child often construes the deception against himself as though he was in some way responsible, and the guilt often endures for a lifetime.

Some of the deepest wounds and most difficult to heal are caused by abuse. This can be physical, emotional, or sexual. It can occur at any age. Today in the news media much attention has been given to child abuse and spouse battering revealing to the public how alarmingly common such incidents are. The harm done is much more serious than the physical damage. Low self-esteem, a burden of guilt and shame, a sense of powerlessness over one's own life, and a fear to trust love or make personal commitments to another will last until wound healing results in forgiveness.

When I listen to people speak about their hurts, there is often a reluctance to face or admit just who it was who hurt them. Often they will preface it with some statement like, "I must have done something wrong," or "I don't know what it was I did but . . . ," or "Maybe he/she thought they were doing the right thing." This effort to excuse those who hurt them frequently stems from the uncomfortable reality that their offenders are precisely the people from whom they had a right to expect love, nourishing care, comfort, and understanding. The finger, of course, points to parents or parent substitutes. The list then ranges out from family, relatives, friends, teachers, clergy, coworkers, employers, people of other ethnic backgrounds or social strata, and total strangers. The list also includes such impersonal organizations as hospitals, schools, the Church, governments, and finally embraces the victims themselves and even God.

Not unexpectedly the wounds inflicted by those closest to us are the most painful, lasting, and traumatic. When we were children they were the ones we turned to, our primary educators. Often we did not even know that we were being abused or mistreated. As I was told by one woman whose mother forced her to sit on a chair in the corner of the kitchen for hours each day, "I thought that was what all children had to do." Another woman whose father forced her, when she was four years old, to drink whiskey with him in his drunken sprees said, "I thought I was being naughty because I tried to spit it out." A young man who was sexually abused by his father for three years, along with his brother and sister, told me, " We were surprised to find out from our friends that all fathers did not do this." These kinds of treatment, only later realized by the victim to be evil, often result in a confusing love/hate relationship with the offending parent.

The way our parents treated us (and, in a similar way, our teachers and church people) naturally became the foundation upon which our adult lives stood (or tottered). Lives are easily twisted at the pliable stage of childhood and "values'" formed which adhere to our very bones. Children adjust to mistreatment the best they can. Their "solutions" are sometimes useful for the original situation, but then they carry out these same solutions, now as inappropriate or even psychotic behavior, in adult situations that trigger them off.

A recent much-celebrated trial of two young men who killed their abusive parents shows an "adult" reaction to childhood molestation. Murder is usually not one of the options available to a child's physical or mental equipment. Children react in childish ways using the only defensive mechanisms they know. These are most often instinctive and take the forms of withdrawal, physical or mental, seeking interior consolations by way of an elaborate fantasy life, stifling any forms of communication, not reaching out for help even when badly needed, finding refuge in eating or any other pain killers available to them.

Perhaps most common of all, low self-esteem is the fruit of early and frequent childhood abuse. A low opinion of self is bred into such children. They see themselves as inferior to others and so avoid new relationships or even continuing with old ones. They have a preset mentality when beginning any new task, " I can't do this. It's too much for me. I'll fail in this as in everything else." Such ideas, of course, become self-fulfilling prophecies that often endure for an unhappy lifetime.

At this point I would like to offer a tool that may be of some help to those who have vivid memories of childhood abuse or even of a single, powerful incident of injustice, misunderstanding, loneliness, or rejection that still lives on in them. No doubt everyone of us fits into this category. We are all familiar with the concept that the child-we-were still lives on within us. So we are two people: the child with all his/her joys and sorrows, reactions and prejudices, fantasies and fears; and the adult who lives with whatever his/her adult reactions are to those childhood experiences as mature responses or triggered reactions.

Call to mind some one incident in your childhood when you were alone, without comfort, even unjustly treated (or even a general sense of that, if it was very common for you).

Picture yourself as vividly as you can. perhaps exiled to your room or fleeing to your special "private place." Recapture the feeling of loss, abandonment, rejection, or grief. Feel it, allow it to surface. It is still there.

Next, as the mature adult that you are (or the maturer person, at least) with all your understanding of how that child feels (stronger and more accurate than any other person could possibly have), go to that suffering child and offer him/her adult understanding, solace, and comfort that the child needs and that only you can understand and give. Speak genuine words of comfort and compassion, hold the child, hug him/her. Do not stop until you feel that the child is responding and finally comforted.

This is more than an imaginary scenario. The child is real, the adult is real and knows the child intimately, knows what the child needs and how to give it and, at this point, is the only one who is able to offer comfort and understanding. It is not too late. It is never too late. Try it!

7
What Do You Deserve?

One would have to be a loving parent, a poet, an orator, a priest, a teacher, a psychiatrist, and a faithful friend to describe with any justice what a given individual deserves. We were created and called to a loving service of God, one another, and ourselves. In theory, at least, the potential is there. We are given parents to bring us into existence, to nurture and cherish us. We are given a supportive society with a government supposedly existing only for our well-being, safety, freedom, and pursuit of happiness. We are introduced into a church community to teach us by word and example what it means to be a loving and beloved brother or sister and a child of God. We enter an educational system to be taught and encouraged to the fullness of our potentiality how to become the best human being we can be. We learn—again, at least in theory—how our particular talents can be developed to best serve others and satisfy our own deepest aspirations. We are taught and encouraged to enter into a professional world where we can contribute to society, as best we can, the fruits of our talents, and where we are adequately compensated with at least some kind of frugal comfort and security. Our health, mental and physical, is a matter of social and even public concern. We marry a partner who complements our own abilities, fills our personal needs, and supports our legitimate ambitions. Finally after a fulfilled and satisfying lifetime of loving and being loved, we are called to enter "into the kingdom prepared for you since the beginning of time."

What is your reaction as you read this? Is it sarcasm, skepticism, regret, amusement, incredulity, or even a kind of bemused hope? We were created to love, and everything else was created to make love possible. This ideal description of the human calling is only a concrete application of what love should be and what love should do.

Certainly it is unrealistic if it is to be taken in every one of its details. However, which ones would you drop as being not in accord with the love we have a right to expect and the loving service that should follow from that love? We certainly have a right to strive for all of these things, to reach out for them and even to expect them. "Well," you may say, "I believe in all of these things and would like to have them and contribute to others the same love and loving service, but there are imperfections and imperfect people in our world who make it impossible . What can I do?"

I have a friend whose father was an old Yankee farmer from New Hampshire. When my friend left the farm to "seek his fortune," his father's parting advice was, "My son, if you ever need a helping hand, you will find it at the end of your arm."

Yes, we live in an imperfect world. Often, when we ask for an egg, we are handed a stone, and when we ask for bread, we are given a scorpion. But no matter how young or old we are, we have a right to a future and the "pursuit of happiness" (even, it should be noted, a constitutional right if we are Americans!). This will not be handed to us. We have to reach for it with the helping hand at the end of our own arm.

All right, so when you were a child you received abuse instead of comfort, rejection instead of warm acceptance, hatred or indifference in place of love, humiliations instead of encouragement and respect. No one of us is free of this. And so you were launched into adulthood on this shaky foundation. You had to live in a world that was cold, demanding, frightening, threatening, nonsupportive, taking what little you were willing or able to give without appreciation or adequate compensation.

You can change it. You can change yourself and consequently the world you live in. You do need a helping hand, and you will find it at the end of your arm. I am not here forgetting the help of God's grace and the significant help that truly concerned and loving people are wanting to offer you. But even for this you have to reach out. Again the hand that will help you will be your own. This is how God deals with us. Others will aid us only to the degree that they can see or expect a response that only we can give.

Do you want the things you deserve and have a right to? Do you want love and acceptance, friends and supporters, growth and maturity, security and fulfillment? Recognize these wants. Spell them out. See them as possible goals and pursue them. Just making the first single step in this direction extricates you from the lost band of the hopeless and will summon you forward with the attraction of challenge, possibilities, and hope. Only you, with God's grace can initiate the movement towards forgiveness and its subsequent wholeness. Begin the process.

8

The Stages of Forgiveness

Studies have been made of the various stages people go through in the process of forgiveness. While they may vary somewhat in number and in what they are called, they are basically similar. [2] These stages are useful for teaching purposes and do have a foundation in reality, but the actual process is not so well-defined or clear-cut. There are times when we find ourselves in more than one stage, or we may be in one stage in the forgiveness process for one hurt and in another stage for an entirely different painful experience. Also the progression from one stage to another may not be as precise as the theory suggests. It is possible to regress, even on a very temporary basis, and return to an earlier stage for a time before again moving forward.

The important thing to realize is that it is a process, a movement, even if there are possibilities of stopping or slowing down the movement by getting stuck in one stage or another. You will be encouraged by recognizing yourself in

---

[2]   The stages followed here are based on those formulated by Simon and Simon, pp. 32–33. See also Beverly Flanagan, *Forgiving the Unforgiveable* (New York: Macmillan, 1992).

these stages. If you are in one or another of these levels you are in process. We will try to give some tools to help you along, especially if you find yourself tending to get stuck on a particular level.

Be encouraged by the process. The most important thing is to begin. It is the single step that begins the journey—no matter how small or hesitant the steps or long the journey. Be aware also of the help that is available to you. It is really God who initiates the movement towards forgiveness. As God says, "Before they call I will answer; while they are still speaking I will hear" (Is 65:24). God will not do your work for you. God has given you the helping hand on the end of your arm. Instead of saying, "I will solve all your problems; I will bring you to wholeness and forgiveness," God says, "I will come to you and give you myself, and I will take your hand and accompany you on your journey. After all, it is a journey towards me. You are my child and I love you." This is what we mean by saying that God is the Alpha and the Omega, the beginning and the end.

Martin Luther King, Jr., no stranger to the forgiveness process, assures us that the first real step lies with the one hurt. Only the person who has been wronged can initiate the forgiving act. Often it will be the victim of some great hurt, some tortuous injustice, some terrible act of oppression.

The philosophers tell us that what is last in the order of execution is first in the order of intention. This means that some goal or end we have in view (e.g., forgiveness of someone who hurt us) is present to us at the very beginning of our journey and the very reason to begin it. Can you see now how beginning the forgiveness process (and not the actual forgiveness itself) is sufficient reason to allow you "to present your gift at the altar" even if you must say in all honesty, "I am still angry, fearful, and hateful and cannot yet forgive; but I have begun the journey." It is more necessary than ever that you bring your gift (yourself) to the altar and receive from that altar God's gift (God's self) in the Body and Blood of Christ.

The kiss of peace which we give and receive before Communion (which very word means "union with God") is the expression of the beginning (or completion) of the process of forgiveness. The worshipers near us, whom we greet in this kiss, represent all men and women everywhere and of every time. Thus the Body of Christ seeks union with the Body of Christ with the aid of the Body of Christ.

9

The First Stage:
Claiming The Hurt

Sometimes this is also called the denial stage. Claiming the hurt is hard work. Deception seems to be easier—or even forgetfulness. No one really wants to claim something that is painful. When you claim something, you make it your own and admit that it is yours. Not only do you have to claim your hurts and admit them, you also have to examine what that hurt has done to your life, your rights, and your expectations for wholeness and happiness. You also have to look squarely at what that hurt may continue to do in your life if it is not healed.

There is that in us that obscures the reality and the clear remembrance of past hurts. Our pride is reluctant to admit how deeply we have been affected and how much of our life has been changed for the worse as a result. Hurts are painful to face so we try almost naturally to look away from them. The memory of hurts increases or prolongs the pain, so we try to forget them. If we can't forget, we minimize the memory and deliberately or indeliberately try to lessen the impact, present and past, of our injuries. If there truly is something of our own fault in the injury, we may try to obscure our guilt in the matter or, perversely, increase it so that we blame ourselves for a cruel injury, perpetrated by someone we love (and hate?).

We try to make sense of our hurts. Children especially, who are used to accepting everything from the hands of significant adults, will try to manufacture reasons—often to the detriment of their self-esteem and the increase of their guilt—so that their hurts can make some sense. It is often not "sense" to children to recognize that some adults are just careless, deranged, or indifferent to them.

Even if your explanation is irrational to others, you have to invent or revise your concepts of morality and justice. You need some kind of interpretation to explain your hurt, and then you go on to live according to these invested (and false) concepts, thus distorting your own life and the lives of those dependent upon you or close to you. The only way you can discover the real reason for your wounds is to talk with the person who inflicted them. This is often impossible, so you try to make sense of them from your own perspectives. You must try to look reality squarely in the face and keep yourself fully aware of it no matter how frightening or threatening the confrontation may be.

You must honestly (and painfully) know precisely what your injuries are and who inflicted them. What is it exactly that needs to be healed? How has it affected your life adversely? What would you be like if it had not happened, or if you were not still bleeding from those wounds?

Accepting your injury means accepting *your* injury and not those of other people, no matter how closely associated. A young man once told me that he could possibly forgive his father for sexually molesting him, but he could never forgive him for abusing his younger brother and sister. While the matter is not totally irrelevant, it is not his problem to forgive the hurts others received. They must deal with that.

Although we are not our wounds, they are a part of what and who we are and who we will be in the future. They have had a great part to play in shaping our lives thus far and will continue to do so. We hope it will not be the wounds that will influence our future but the scars certainly will. Yet we know that scars are stronger than unwounded flesh. We must accept the wound if we are to treat it for healing—and the scar which results from it.

It is necessary to know, not only whom to forgive, but what it is we forgive. We have to recognize the extent of our injuries. We have to see what they have done to our trust, our sense of justice, our self-esteem, and our ability to relate freely to our world. It is not just the act of wounding itself that the perpetrator is responsible for (and must be forgiven for) but all of its repercussions.

It is inevitable that our memories and our interpretations will be either inaccurate or unclear. This pertains to more recent hurts as well as to injuries of many years standing. We simply have to deal with them as frankly and as honestly as we can, sparing neither ourselves nor others. If we truly remembered and understood *everything* (as God does), perhaps forgiveness would not even be necessary. When we see the stupidity, the weakness, the selfishness and the folly of humanity—which includes ourselves—it will make forgiving not only more realistic but even a bit easier.

Denial can take many forms. We can deny that we were hurt at all. We can claim that we were really wounded but that it wasn't as bad as it seems. We can say that we were hurt and it was bad but that we have gotten over it (you haven't gotten over it if you have not forgiven).

We do have to admit we have and have had enemies, people who have hurt us. They must be identified as clearly as possible if we are to know whom we are to forgive. Once they are identified, we have the opportunity to make our Christian commitment real. After all, what place does the gospel have in our lives if it is not to deal with our wounding and forgiving one another. Is not the gospel summed up in the words of Jesus, "By this let all know you are my disciples, that you have love for one another" (Jn 13:35).

A one-liner coming from the novel and later the movie *Love Story* states, "Love means never having to say you're sorry." This sentimental nonsense became very popular and was embellished on sweat shirts, banners, and badges. If love never offends, it never has to say it is sorry, but when it does offend (and it will) it must apologize and accept the apology (forgive). Rather should we cherish another one-liner which says, "Love means being the first to say you're sorry," and we might add, "Love means being prompt to accept such sorrow."

What are some tools to help you to enter into the first stage of forgiveness, claiming the hurt, and how can you facilitate your progress so that you do not get stuck in this state? Try writing a letter to the one who hurt you. Explain how you felt then and now. Tell him/her how your life has been influenced by the injury and what it does to you presently. Express your feelings, your indignation, the reasons why you find it so hard (impossible?) to forgive. Then write another letter—this might be the most useful tool for you—to yourself pretending it is from the perpetrator. Make this letter an apology, together with any possible explanation that could help you understand where he/she was coming from when they harmed you. To write one or both of these letters is to claim your injury and name the blame. This is a good start.

If your injurer is someone who is still alive and if you (or he/she) has severed all communication, it is important, (if you can) to let them know that you are open (if you are) to the possibility of communication, especially if they are not apt, at the present moment, to respond to any efforts at personal contact. This could be done by just sending a Christmas or birthday card—even one with just a printed message and your signature. This will let the injurer know that you would not reject any efforts to restore a relationship. Then, pray. Pray for your injurer if you can—even if it is only for God to let him/her be aware of the depth and extent of the harm done. If you can, pray further for them to seek forgiveness themselves, or if they are dead, to receive God's forgiveness. If you cannot yet pray for your injurer then pray for yourself. Pray that you might be receptive to God's call to begin the process toward your own freedom and wholeness. You can only start from where you are. You can only do what is possible for you right now. That will be enough.

10
The Second Stage:
Guilt

When we get through the denials and accept the fact that the injury was real and had a negative influence on our life and we are able to face squarely just who was responsible for it, we will move on to the second stage in the forgiveness process. From this point on, I am going to refer to it as the wholeness process because that is really what we are seeking. The forgiveness follows from the healing of our wounds, which will be our wholeness.

In this second stage, we seek for some explanation for what was done to us. It is only natural, in a sense, that we look to ourselves for a reason. This is all that we know. When, as is often the case, the perpetrator is someone close to us, we are reluctant to put the blame entirely on them. We adopt the attitude: there must have been something I did to provoke the injury. It must be my fault, maybe even all my fault.

I counseled a woman who was gang-raped many years ago. She was stuck in this stage. As far as I could tell she was completely innocent, but she was still asking herself: What could I have done differently to avoid it? What did I do to provoke it? Was it the way I dressed? How I walked? Should I have struggled more? Screamed louder? Am I just a bad person? Did

I deserve what happened to me? If I had gone to school that day this would not have happened. I am at fault. I am no good. Coming from this stage, that woman spent four years as a prostitute. She hated it but could not see herself as doing anything better. This, she thought, was where she belonged.

Sometimes, of course, the issues are much more complicated. This makes self-blame all the easier, for example, in a divorce situation or a job disappointment. No one is perfect and there are two sides to each story, but personal responsibility in this stage is exaggerated beyond reason. It is also a form of copping out. If the victim is the guilty one, then there is no one else to blame and consequently to forgive. We can just stay where we are and bleed.

A priest who was blatantly mistreated by his bishop, and who had every right (but no due process) to extricate himself from the situation, spent years agonizing after his decision to leave the ministry. Was he after all called to suffer injustice with Christ? Did he violate his commitment to obedience by not suffering further the unfair pain and hurt? Was he responsible for scandal? Maybe, he reasoned, it would have gotten better if he stayed?

Being stuck in self-blame, he began to show the reactions common to that stage. He became a perfectionist in his job. If he did everything just right, no one (especially his bosses) would be able to find fault with him. In fact, the truth of the matter was that he was fired for being too unyielding in his perfectionism. His mind became like a videotape where he played certain negative scenarios over and over again, almost as though one of the replays might change the past and it would be different. He was frequently depressed, developed colitis and migraines, and eventually sought escape in the forgetfulness of alcohol. His self-esteem was so destroyed that he gave up altogether. Any new endeavor he tried was defeated from the start because he "just knew" he could not succeed. He dressed, acted, lived, and became a defeated man.

What can you do to move out of this self-blame, low-esteem level? The first helpful thing is to recognize the stage for what it is. If you can recognize and understand what you are doing, you can decide to do something about it. Secondly, the exercise of comforting the inner child described previously can be a great help. Know that you deserve comfort, consolation, and understanding and that you are capable of giving it to yourself. This is just the opposite of self-blame and wallowing in low self-esteem. Consider some practical things that you could do for the child to help him/her. Perhaps a gift, a movie, space to cry—anything to show that he/she is worthwhile, even special. Do that for yourself. Somebody once told me, "I send myself flowers!" Do it!

In your prayer try to think and talk over with God your great worth as his child. Remind God (and hence yourself) that God is on your side. You and God can do anything! See what African Americans did to bolster their self-esteem. Instead of denigrating themselves as persecuted members of a minority race, they declared that black was beautiful and supported themselves by affirming their brother/sisterhood. See what some members of the gay community did. Instead of accepting the inferior status that others had imposed on them (wounded them), they formed organizations (such as Dignity) which affirmed their self-worth.

11
The Third Stage:
Victim

You have accepted the reality of your hurt, have faced (at least internally) its perpetrator, and have accepted the fact that you were not responsible for your wounds. They were unjustly inflicted upon you. Your next "logical" step is victimhood. It was done, it hurt, you did not do it, someone else did. It was beyond your control. You were helpless, victimized. Everyone should feel sorry for you. You wallow in feeling sorry for yourself. The signs of being a victim are obvious. You are depressed, listless, down-trodden, isolated, not understood, and bitter. You tend to find your consolations in forms of narcotization—drugs (prescription medicine?), alcohol, overeating, television, chocolate, workshop after workshop, gambling, and so forth. As you wallow in your misery, you feel justified in your indulgences and your subtle passive–aggressive stances. You will come late to appointments and then be surprised at how it may bother others. You will forget things like errands and small inconvenient commitments.

At times the victim will display anger, not at himself or at his woundedness, but at those around him. Scathing criticism, forms of racism, even child abuse and spouse-beating or berating can be an expression of this victim stage.

People in this stage become the walking wounded. They lose their individuality and their personality to become identified with their hurts. They see themselves only in terms of their pain and hurts. They will usually describe themselves in those terms: "I am the daughter of alcoholic parents, an abused child (even as adults, they will say this), or a victim of incest.

Self-esteem, already low from the self-blame stage, takes a further downward plunge. They become like Job sitting on his dung heap bemoaning his suffering before the world and rubbing salt into his wounds. So convinced do they become at the hopelessness of their misery, that they will not even hear helpful advice or encouragement. Nothing can help them. Nobody can do anything for them because no one can understand their pain. Their theme song is, "Nobody knows the trouble I've seen, nobody knows my sorrow."

This kind of identification with wounds and suffering can, for some people, be very dangerous. When someone identifies with his sorrows, when they become their pains, then the only way to get rid of the pain is to get rid of themselves—suicide!

The victim stage is not difficult to identify. It even serves particular purposes as long as it is just a stage and not a permanent lifestyle. It is not unlike the grieving process. It gives what is due to past hurts. It can, however, perpetuate itself by becoming itself a new kind of pain—the pain of bemoaning and regretting pain. Sometimes when injuries are inflicted on a child, the child is too preoccupied or too much engaged in mere survival to indulge in the luxury of feeling sorry for himself. Some of this pity is necessary, and it will have its day.

The victim stage is a cry for help. It is an appeal for sympathy, comfort, and consolation but an oddly disguised one. The victim, seeking consolations in self-indulgence or in hitting back at innocent bystanders, will not receive or accept genuine comfort or sympathetic advice. Eventually people will give up on such victims and cease bestowing the very consolations their clinging victimization was put on to obtain.

The victim stage allows us to express the sorrow, regret, and opposition we would like to have expressed when the wounds were inflicted. It is a way to finally get the sympathetic attention we should have received when we were first wounded. What must be kept in mind with all of this, however, is that these justifications for the victim stage are only temporary. For some people the victim stage becomes a lifestyle, lasting many years or even a lifetime. We must avoid this kind of getting stuck, thus becoming what we think we are. What can we do to get out of this stage and move along with our life and our wholeness process?

An obvious step in this direction is to join a support group. A search through the notices in the daily newspaper will demonstrate that there are as many kinds of support groups as there are wounds. It is healthy and helpful to see that your hurts are not unique, that there are others who understand what you went through and can sympathize with you. It is also good for you to see people with similar tragic backgrounds who are moving on with their lives. To talk about your pain constructively and instructively (helping others) is what you need to step out of the mire of wallowing self-pity and bitterness.

Recognize your assets, your good points, your blessings. Draw up a list of them and post it in some convenient place so you can add to it day by day as new things happen or as you remember past blessings. You are more than your sorrows. You need to make the effort necessary to escape your pessimistic mind set.

One of the setbacks of the victim stage is a depressive low energy. Do things for yourself, for others. Start slowly and with little things. Experience the lift you can get by getting out of yourself and helping someone else.

Avoid what I call "worm theology." This is a kind of spiritual justification to allow you to wallow in misery and self-pity by giving a theological justification to it. In St. Mark's Gospel (15:34), he describes Jesus on the cross quoting the first line of Psalm 22: "My God, my God, why have you forsaken me?" When we turn to Psalm 22 and read it in its entirety, we can understand that St. Mark is telling us that this psalm is a prophecy of Jesus' death and resurrection. Not only does it describe the events of Jesus' passion, but, by quoting the first line, St. Mark wants us to understand that this psalm became the prayer of Jesus just before his death. In verses 6 and 7 of this prayer then, we can recognize the complaint (victim stage statement) of Jesus in the words from which I take the phrase "worm theology": "But I am a worm and not a man, scorned by men and despised by the people. All who see me mock me." Jesus recognized himself as a victim. But it is important to recognize that he did not stop there but proceeded from victimhood to wholeness and gratitude. This becomes clear when we read the entire psalm as the prayer of Jesus on the cross. From verse 23, "You who fear the Lord, praise him," until the end, he praises the Father for what will happen in the future as the story of his goodness goes through the world and even into the future. "Posterity will serve him; future generations will be told about the Lord" (verse 30).

Jesus, through Psalm 22 could give a theological justification to this suffering because he knew and desired that somehow it would end in the Father's glory. His victimhood was not something to wallow in as an expression of self-pity as a permanent state ("worm theology"), but to pass through to greater things.

In your prayer accept your past and its pain. What else can you do? The past is the only certain manifestation of God's will we have. God's will for the future is not a reliving of past sorrows but a new horizon stemming from God's promises, God's love and graciousness, and God's helping hand which, remember, is at the end of your arm. Always remember that you are more than your wounds.

12

The Fourth Stage: Anger

"I was hurt," we say in the victim stage. "I was wounded. They (he/she) did this to me." When finally we are able to add, "But I'll be damned if I will put up with it or with its pain in my life any longer," we have advanced to the anger stage. It represents a real step forward.

Unlike the anger, repressed or active, of the victim stage, the anger of the fourth stage is actually positive and forward looking. It is not concerned with getting back but with getting ahead. It involves a definite thrust out of morbid, self-centered, self-pitying lamentation into a vigorous, outer-directed energy that declares: "This will never happen to me again. I am neither helpless nor hopeless and I absolutely refuse to be defined by my wounds and sufferings." There can be seen even something God-like in this stance. God defined Godself to Moses as "I Am Who Am," i.e., I can be defined by nothing outside myself or by nothing that happens to me but only by who I say that I am.

In this state, we refuse to be victimized any longer. We thrust ourselves forward out of the mire we had been embogged in and begin to look around ourselves. We may not yet know where we are going or even how to get there, but we are moving. Most of the fear is gone and even many of the unhappy reactions that the fear triggered. Instead of lamenting our mistreatment, we use our energy in doing something about it. It is like Job getting off his dung heap, taking a shovel, and clearing it aside. This is a needed activity in the forgiveness and wholeness process. Forgiveness cannot be something we casually place over a churning fear throbbing beneath.

In the place of self-pity, we now substitute outrage. We can use this constructively if we choose. It need not be destructive. If we choose to direct this energy toward vengeance, it will destroy our injurers and ourselves. If we direct it toward positive goals, it will be decisive in moving on toward wholeness. To use it for the sake of revenge is to lose our freedom and to allow what happened to us in the past to dictate our present and our future. Vengeful aggression destroys its perpetrator even before it affects the object of its hate. We can observe this kind of anger socially in the Black Rage movement and in the Jewish reaction to persecutions by their oft-repeated statement: Never Again!

There are special problems for certain people when they are ready to enter into the anger stage. These are the people who have taken to heart the rather black-and-white type of morality that says that anger is wrong. Of course, it is not. It is only what we do with anger that may or may not be wrong. Anger directed towards revenge is wrong. Anger used as an energetic thrust towards future freedom and wholeness is good. Some of us fear our anger because it is so deep and strong that we dread what will happen if it is unleashed. Some, perhaps, have also seen, i.e., in their earlier years, what anger can do and, indeed, what it did do to them or to those around them. A child who has been beaten by an angry parent or a spouse who has been battered as an object of anger will find it difficult to see anger as a positive force.

An angry person lives in an angry world. This is the result of projection by which you disown you own angry feelings and attribute them to others. It is a way of not admitting or accepting your own anger. You can also repress your anger. Repression involves the subconscious blocking of angry emotions from your conscious awareness. This happens as a reflex action. The anger thus repressed will express itself in devious ways often difficult to recognize. It can manifest itself as anxiety or psychosomatically as ulcers, colitis, or headaches. It can also be unconsciously projected as hatred of women or men, or as ethnic prejudice. You can also, of course, deliberately suppress your anger. This is a conscious exclusion of unwanted feelings. It can be good or bad depending upon your motives and how you do it.

Anger is better expressed than suppressed. There are tools that have proven useful in the expression of anger. Some of the things that we do or are tempted to do to express anger aggressively can be controlled as a deliberate expression harmlessly activated. An angry person slams doors, inflicts physical or verbal harm on others, or breaks things. I recall going through some angry feelings during my monastic novitiate. My confessor suggested that I take an axe and chop down some trees in an area of the woods that needed thinning. Thus my anger was expressed constructively. I remember a cartoon in *Peanuts* where Linus stood on the beach with a pile of stones next to him. He would hurl them one at a time into the water saying, "This is for wife beaters, this is for hungry children, this is for drunken drivers," and so on. We can do something similar, beat pillows, go to a private place and scream. This can be useful on a temporary basis and harms no one. It does allow the steam to escape even though it will probably build itself up again.

A more decisive and lasting way to deal with anger is to examine its sources and treat not the symptoms, but the cause. We start by trying to discover the cause. When someone or something triggers your anger, it does not tell you much about that person or thing, but it can be a mine of useful information about yourself. What does your anger tell you about yourself? Why does this particular situation or person trigger your anger? The answer is not outside you but within. What in your own life or background is being touched? As Jesus put it, "What goes into a man's mouth does not make him 'unclean', but what comes out of his mouth, that is what makes him 'unclean.' . . . But the things that come out of the mouth come from the heart, and these make a man 'unclean.' For out of the heart come evil thoughts, murder, adultery, sexual immorality, theft, false testimony, slander. These are what make a man 'unclean.'" (Mt 15:10, 18–20)

There is a particular way to approach anger that may be helpful. When we recognize the arousal of angry feelings, we can attribute them in general to one of three causes. We are presently being threatened in one (or more) of three ways. Our need for security, our desire for approval, or our need to control a situation has been threatened. Examine the immediate internal cause of your anger. You will usually find that you can easily recognize how it touches upon one of these three issues: security, control or need for approval. This is a way to get in touch with our wounds because whichever button is being pushed, security, control, or approval, goes back to some incident(s) of our early experience.

Once you decide which button it is that is being pushed, you then can make a statement like this: "I am getting angry because my son forgot to shovel the walk. Why does this make me angry? Is it because my security is threatened? No. Is it my need for approval? No. Is it my desire to control? Certainly!"

The next thing you ask yourself is: "Am I willing to give up my desire to control (approve, to be secure) in this particular incident—which is the cause of my anger. You can do this simply by willing it. It does not mean you are letting your son escape his duties. It does mean that you are enabling yourself to correct him without anger. Because you want him to do the right thing and not because he is triggering for you a control issue. So you just tell yourself: "I am angry because I want control over this situation. But my anger will actually do just the opposite. If I express it, I will loose control. So I do willingly and deliberately surrender my desire to control this situation."

Now, as you no longer have a desire to control, there is nothing here to trigger your anger. You can then calmly proceed to deal with your son's neglect without using it as an outlet for your own issues.

There is a reasonable theory that we each possess a vast reservoir of undifferentiated emotional energy within us. This energy can surface in any one of any number of emotions or feelings. We do have some control over how these feelings are released. The stronger and more energetic emotions are actually closely related in terms of their energetic power, e.g., anger, hatred, and love! They represent energy coming from this reservoir which we direct into particular closely related channels expressive of love or hatred or anger. It is up to us what we do with them.

Anger has its place. But if we do not rule it, it will rule us. That is not its place. For the wholeness process to be genuinely healing and hence forgiving, we must allow ourselves to feel the hurt and express our anger. We need an awareness of the pain that we have and the energetic thrust to do something constructive for its healing.

There is further information on the method for dealing with anger constructively—what I call being "free to love"—described in detail in chapter 28 of this book, on the subject of vulnerability.

13
The Final Stage: Wholeness

We begin to deal with our wounds by denying or minimizing them. When we finally do face them squarely and recognize the ones who inflicted them, we move on to the next step. This usually involves trying to excuse the perpetrator and blaming ourselves for causing or, at least, not stopping, the original wounds. When we are able to cease the self-blame, we begin to feel sorry for ourselves and to wallow in a mud hole of self-pity, bitterness, and recrimination. The next step is anger. We determine that we will do something about what happened to us and move forward with our lives. We stop rubbing salt in our wounds, and we actively seek healing. This leads us to the final stage, wholeness.

For each of the stages there is a danger of getting stuck. Sometimes a person spends years, or even a lifetime, in one of the first four steps, even regressing on occasion to one or the other. We have given some tools that may be helpful for moving on in our lives and to avoid regression or stagnation. One of the best tools is a recognition of where we are. To journey towards a goal is difficult if we do not know where we are starting from or our progress at any given point.

In his *Handbook to Higher Consciousness*, Ken Keyes says, "The world tends to be your mirror. A peaceful person lives in a peaceful world. An angry person creates an angry world. . . . An unfriendly person should not be surprised when he/she meets only people who sooner or later respond in an unfriendly way."[3] So the environment which we create hinders us—or it can help us. It also follows that a wholesome person creates and abides in a wholesome world, and a forgiving person lives in a forgiving world.

We are now at the final step in the wholeness process. The place where forgiveness happens—as a by-product, as it were, of our healing. Realizing our hurt and our hurter, knowing what we did (or did not do) to facilitate the wounding, having mourned our suffering and determined to do something about it, we now proceed to do it.

We are now coming out at the top. We are claiming our right to wholeness and happiness. We refuse to let our lives be ruled by past mistakes, our own or those of others. You are the master of your fate, the captain of your soul. You are alive and well and living in your world. In one *Peanuts* cartoon, Charlie Brown is bemoaning his wretched life as usual. Lucy takes him firmly by the shoulders and says: "Charlie Brown, look around you. Do you see your world? Is this the world you live in? Do you have any other? Then live in it!!" And this is what we now do.

No doubt we enter (re-enter?) our world with a limp and some scars, but we are now willing to recognize these as badges of success. They represent where we were, what happened to us to bring us to here, and where we will be in the future.

We recognize that we have damaged ourselves and others and we feel a healthy guilt. It is not arising out of some murky

---

3   Ken Keyes, *Handbook to Higher Consciousness* (St. Mary, Ky.: Living Love Publications, 1975), 29.

subconscious, triggered by unexpected and misunderstood events, but comes from a real and conscious look at our past actions. We can and are willing to do something about them. A forgiving person lives in a forgiving world. We have a real and genuine sorrow for opportunities missed but we recognize that there is no point in gazing back on the past when we can focus our sights on the present and the future. We did what we could, and we will do what we can.

There is a tool here that will help us to move on even further. If there is one thing that is true about our past, it is that it happened. It is real, and it is over. As a past, there is absolutely nothing that we can do about it. We can, of course, prevent it from becoming our future but that still does not change the past. It did happen. It will always be our past. There is nothing else to do but to accept it. There is a real sense in which we can say that our past, no matter how unfortunate, is perfect. It is as it is. It could not possibly be any better. Therefore I accept it, use it for any benefits I can gain from it, and move forward.

At this point and whenever unpleasant incidents from the past impinge on your conscious memory—embrace them. Let your prayer be the prayer of Jesus who is the Eternal Amen to the Father. "For all that shall be, Amen."

Who are you now? You will begin to identify your real self. A child of God, a man or woman with a real appreciation for yourself and your life. As a person who does make a difference. Yes, your past happened. You did suffer. But that is not your identity. It is something that happened to you and which you are able to put to your advantage and perhaps that of others.

And now as you realize that your wounds are healing or healed, you begin to say: "I truly have nothing to be angry about and nobody to be angry against." This is when you cross the threshold of forgiveness. You can recognize now that your forgiveness, an expression of your wholeness, is your way to fairness in an otherwise unfair world. You realize that you could not truly forgive in response to a command, even from God. Real forgiveness cannot be squeezed out of a sense of duty, it is given freely or not at all. It is neither a power play nor a manipulation, but an act of love.

Your injurers are also free—at least, as far as you are concerned. The perpetrators still have to deal with their part in their transgression, but they don't owe you anything. You are not dependent on what someone else does for you just as you are no longer dependent on what someone else did to you. You can now freely release them of all personal debts. It is quite another question as to whether or not you allow them to make amends for their own personal needs, the requirements of justice, or the promptings of love.

Just as you now realize that you are not your wounds and you are more than a victim, perhaps you will also be ready to recognize that your injurer is more than a perpetrator of wounds. He/she is a human being, a child of God with his/her own sorrows, sins, pains, wounds, regrets, and needs. Perhaps you can now begin to accept him/her as such.

It is also at this point that you may look to reconciliation. You may want to initiate it or, at least, open the way towards it. This is not something that should be attempted prematurely. You must feel ready. Reconciliation can be made with the dead through prayer and also through the compassion exercise I will describe in chapter 25 of this book.

Possibly now you could write a forgiving letter. In some ways it does not even matter whether or not you actually send it. Sometimes that is not even possible. But the positive, clarifying action of putting your forgiveness in concrete terms will be a great help to you. Notice how you feel as you plan and write the letter. Can you do it with some ease, without feelings of shame, anger, or recrimination? If you can, then you know that your forgiveness is genuine and total.

It is time to move on. Do positive things with your life. Be significant to others by your love, concern, attention, and service. Make changes. Do new things for yourself, for your health, your interests, your education, you recreation, your general well-being. Live in the wholesome world of your own making. It is not a world without pain, but the pain can be redemptive. It is not a world without sorrow, but know that sorrow is not an evil but a proof of love.

PART TWO

Nine
Travelers

14
The Centers

The following chapters are based on the nine personality profiles as illustrated by the Enneagram system of personality types, sources about which can be found in the bibliography. Somewhere among these nine travelers you will find yourself. No doubt you will find something of yourself in each of them, but most probably a single one will stand out as embodying your basic personality. This is by no means a full treatment of the personality, such as the Enneagram offers, but merely a general overview with an emphasis on how each type responds to the journey from wounds to wholeness and forgiveness.

It will be helpful, before we treat of the nine personality types as individuals, to look at the three centers out of which they operate (three types to each center). A center is a basic approach to reality, a way of knowing, a method of interpreting ourselves and our environment. In fact, even as we will find something of ourselves in each of the nine personalities, we will also recognize that we use the approach of each of the three centers. However, one of the three will dominate our way of learning, knowing, understanding, and responding to the realities we confront.

Probably everybody has seen, at one time or another, the movie classic, *The Wizard of Oz*. This serves us as a very apt metaphor for the three centers. Dorothy, a little girl, has been misplaced by a tornado into the fantastic land of Oz. Her one great desire is to go home again, to Kansas. So she sets out on a journey to the city of Oz to see the great Wizard who, it is claimed, knows everything and who will tell her how to get home.

Dorothy is really seeking wholeness. She wants to be where she belongs, where she will learn and grow under the loving and nurturing care of Auntie Em. Her true home is not Oz, where she was violently transported by a catastrophic accident (a tornado), a painful experience!

It is worth noting that when the great Wizard of Oz turns out to be a phony, Dorothy is told by the good witch that she had all along the ability to return home—the ruby slippers—the very shoes she wore to travel to the city of Oz, and which were the foundations of her journey.

The whole Dorothy is a person who views the world through her three centers of knowledge: her heart, her head, and her body. These are the three characters whom she comes in contact with on the yellow brick road and who accompany her on the journey towards wholeness.

The scarecrow is her brain center; the tin man, her heart center; and the lion, her body center. Please note that each of these centers is seeking something from the Wizard that he thinks he lacks but which actually is the very thing he is most in possession of. The scarecrow seeks a brain, but he is the one, throughout the journey, who comes up with plans, whenever they are needed, for safety and progress. The tin man seeks a heart, yet he is constantly rusting up by his tearful emotional and sympathetic response to people he meets. The lion seeks courage but nonetheless is the hero of the three when facing the dangers of their common adventure.

This illustrates a principle very important in the Enneagram approach. Your virtue is your vice. Your vices are actually an exaggeration or underdoing of your innate abilities, your virtues. To find your strengths, then, you must examine your weaknesses. This is shown also by the Wizard's response to their requests. He does not give them a brain, a heart, or courage. Rather he gives them something that assures them that they already have a brain (a diploma), a heart (a ticking clock), and courage (a medal for bravery).

We are all equipped with these three centers but, for each of us, one of them dominates, another of them is fairly well developed, and a third is deficient. The dominant one, whichever it may be, is in charge even when we use one of the others. We must seek a balance by learning to use properly all three centers if we are to be successful on our journey towards wholeness and forgiveness.

The Christine doctrine of Original Sin teaches us that we have somehow been wounded by the very fact of coming into existence. While God created all things good, and even saw "man" whom God created as "very good," nonetheless, as the fall of Adam and Eve teaches us, we are all affected, wounded, distorted, and hurt by the very fact of our entering into the human race. The image of God according to which we are made has been marred. Our life's journey is to restore that image by grace, through the perfect image, Christ.

Each of the nine personality types of the Enneagram theory has been wounded in a different way and reflects that woundedness throughout life by certain ways of responding to internal reality. Up until now, we have been speaking of the process of forgiveness, as it deals with particular hurts, offenses, and wounds we have experienced in our lives and which we specifically remember—both the wound and the perpetrator. Now we will look at deeper wounds, stemming from our very origins, without neglecting the specific hurts of our lives past, present, or future.

By following the principle that our vice is our virtue and our strength is to be recognized in our weakness, we will look to our own weakest center (our repressed center) for each personality type to discover its particular woundedness and where healing lies. We will recommend certain healing and also prayerful tools to aid in this process. These prayer-tools are described in part three of this book as scriptural meditation, compassion meditation, centering meditation, the process of focusing, and vulnerability.

The following characters are entirely fictitious. Their personalities are true.

15

Mary, the Server

Mary Parker, a psychiatric nurse, is fifty-five years old. Her husband, Tom, sixty, is a tenured professor of economics at the local community college. They have two grown children, both married and living some distance away.

Mary was the only child of a sickly mother. She was devoted to her father, the vice president of the same college where her husband now teaches. Her father was very preoccupied with his job to which his family definitely took second place. He spent long hours at the office, which suited her mother fine so she could spend her time nursing her tension headaches. As a young child, Mary would eagerly await her dad's homecomings, late as they were, and early on learned how to keep his dinner warm and serve it. She was "daddy's little girl," and he often said he did not know who was the first to greet him when he came home, the dog or Mary.

Her mother would often tell her friends around the tea table how she depended on Mary even when Mary was very young. She would bask in this praise and adult admiration and would seek to make herself useful, watching to see if she could anticipate their needs and get even further approval. More and more her mother began to depend on Mary's services in order to indulge in her psychosomatic illnesses.

Unconsciously Mary realized that her own well-being depended on meeting her parents' needs. She learned to anticipate them by being sensitive to her mother's body language or her father's tone of voice. In later childhood Mary would neglect many of the usual childhood occupations, friends, and games, so she could wait upon her mother or anticipate her father's return. She would get upset if anything interfered with her being home to greet her father. It was important for her that he know she was there. As she looks back on her early days, Mary can hardly recall what she did to amuse herself or even remember childhood friends. She vividly remembers, however, being "mother's helper" and "daddy's little girl"!

Because of the professional demands of his job, Mary's father was often distant and even neglectful. This simply made her strive all the harder for his attention, appreciation, and love. She was at times upset by his attitude but grateful when he would notice her. Once when she was quite ill and feverish, she dreaded his return home lest he not approve of her weakness and tried to look cheerful and healthy even at great cost.

As she looks back on it now, Mary has feelings of bitterness towards both of her parents. She feels that they never really appreciated what she did and seldom acknowledged her services. Even today she feels her mother takes her for granted in spite of all she does. She sees the same attitude in her mother-in-law, a patient at the rest home where Mary works. Mary is not one of her fans and is quite outspoken about it.

Mary lives in the worlds of those around her. She has none of her own. Her father died when she was twelve. Overwhelmed by her sense of abandonment, she could not fathom how he could do this to her. Forgiving her father became one of the great tasks of her life.

Mary spent many years in the victim stage of her journey toward wholeness. She was wounded every time her efforts to serve were not appreciated. It took her a long time to recognize this tendency and learn to serve others because of their needs and not, primarily, because of her own.

Sometimes (often) Mary prides herself as being a saintly person. She is interested in others in a self-sacrificing way. In a moment of irritation, her daughter once told her that she smothered her and she had to get away. When both her son and daughter moved away to college and marriage, Mary was lost, confused, and hurt—further wounds that she had to heal in her forgiveness process. She saw this, in some way, as a rejection of herself.

Fortunately Mary had her job. Her patients needed her. Indeed they found her empathetic, warm, and comforting and quickly learned to express their gratitude in small ways that Mary appreciated and needed. There were times, however, when she overdid it, making them dependent upon her. She vaguely recalled doing the same thing with her children. Her daughter would still, on occasion, jokingly refer to Mary as "her Jewish Mother." She still had the apron strings ready to tie someone onto.

Mary met her own insecure and dependent needs by meeting the needs of others. She had no real existence on her own or of her own. She existed only in and for others. Her own needs she rejected. When asked by someone, "Mary, what can I do for you?," she would reply, "What can I do for *you?*" At staff meetings at the rest home, Mary always pours the coffee, adjusts the blinds, and makes everyone comfortable. Her major concern is not, did the meeting accomplish its goals, but did I relate to everyone? If she did, the meeting was a success even it its chief purpose was frustrated.

Mary often thought of her husband as a third child whom she could mother. In fact, she has told friends that she married Tom because " he needed me."

Of the three centers we spoke about, Mary operates chiefly from the heart (the tin man). But in fact, as our strengths are the reverse side of our weaknesses, Mary fears she has no real heart of her own. She suspects this, but still finds her own needs filled not in herself, but in others. She needs others' approval and prides herself in her relationship with significant others in her job and family life.

Alert to meet the needs of others, she is always ready with advice. This can be from a genuine desire to help or from a selfish need to manipulate.

Mary actually needs the victim stage and the sense of loss or abandonment that brings it on. She needs the depression it nourishes to be brought to an awareness of her own lacks and desires. She also needs a bit of the lion in her life, the courage and independence that the instinctual body or gut center will supply. To stand on her own two feet (and not on someone else's), to admit her legitimate needs, and to help herself for a change, will go a long way towards Mary's wholeness. She has to realize that she is neither her wounds nor her relatedness to others but is her own woman. When she is able to do this, she will find her wounds are healed and the by-product of that healing, forgiveness toward herself and others, will take place.

Mary's weakness is pride. She will find her strength in humility. This will cause her to face the nameless fear (wound) and anxiety that underlies her activity and which directs her away from herself. She is afraid that when her veneer of caring for others is stripped away, she will have nothing left.

In her prayer, Mary needs to find the God within. Centering prayer will help her to set aside her outward impulsions and to look inward towards that point at the heart of her being which, she will find, is very real after all (see chapter 26). Mary relates well to all forms of group prayer. She belongs to a prayer group that meets weekly and loves the warmth and intimacy of relating to others on the deep level of prayer. Prayer helps Mary to have a sense of her personal needs and to seek their satisfaction. Any kind of a relational support group will be of great help to her.

The compassion meditation described in chapter 25 is a natural for her. She will relate well to it. She also probably stands in need of comforting the child within described earlier. The process of focusing as described in chapter 27 would also be useful for Mary, whose central way of knowing is through relations and feelings. As her virtues are her vices, as with all of us, she needs to tap her "body knowledge." She usually can get in touch with the pain of past wounds but will see them in terms of the persons who inflicted them. She is also wounded by neglect and a lack of appreciation. Focusing is an ideal way for her to deal with her wounds and to realize that she is more than her feelings.

As Mary matures she finds that she is satisfied to be more of a partner than a servant or a "Jewish mother." She is still sensitive to others needs and seeks to fulfill them, not as a substitute for her own fears and needs, but out of a genuine sense of love and concern for others. The very thing she sought before by responding to others will be given to her only when she reaches the point of relinquishing it.

16
Joe, the Winner

Joe is a used car salesman and a very successful one. He looks, lives, and acts the part. To him success is everything. If he should fail in any endeavor, he will try to hide it even from himself in the appearance of success. Failure is the thing that hurts him the most. He belongs to half-a-dozen clubs, committees, and civic improvement groups. As long as the group succeeds in its goals, Joe will be active and dependable. When he is the leader, which he usually is, the group will generally succeed. If the group fails, Joe will reframe the failure so that it appears to be at least a partial success and then go on to better things.

Joe had two older brothers and was taught and encouraged to be fiercely competitive with them. It was only natural to extend this attitude towards his peers, his classmates, and even his friends. One day he brought home a report card with four A's and one B. Instead of approval, his father demanded, "Why are there not five A's?" Joe was the first in his troop to become an Eagle Scout. His collection of merit badges was based, not on the value of the skills they represented, but on the keeping ahead of the others numerically for the sake of the approval and attention they obtained for him.

Life was a constant upward climb for Joe, and he excelled in scholarship, sports, and social activities. Everything but personal satisfaction. He was never satisfied because there was always something else to win, someone else to beat. In sports he preferred events where he could excel individually. Thus he became a track and swimming star. Although invited to participate, he avoided the baseball team because he knew he could never become captain.

Joe learned early in life to define himself by what he could produce and achieve. The way to love and approval was in a successful performance. If Joe did not always win he knew how to project a winner's image, even it if involved a fancy bit of deception. His goal in high school was to have more credits in the year book descriptions than anyone else. He succeeded and wondered why his victory was so hollow.

Joe had no time for a personal life. He found it easy to maintain an image and change it as often as necessary. He was always wearing a mask of some kind or other and managed to hide even from himself. While others saw Joe as a winner and an achiever, he saw nothing. This pushed him further into his frenetic activity to succeed and to substitute the approval he won for the real love he lacked and craved.

Joe abused his wife, not physically but verbally and by his unreasonable expectations. For years he maintained the facade of a perfect marriage. He coerced his wife into staying with him and living out the role of a happy family life. Two things happened then. His wife, Marge, had had enough, left him, and sued for divorce. At the same time, Joe was running for local political office. His personal life was exposed for what it was, and he suffered a substantial defeat.,

At the time this was the only kind of wound that would hurt Joe. He was used to ignoring his pains and at times even believed in the successful image he projected to the world. There had been rare moments when he suspected that people valued only the good front he put up and not his real self. He would even occasionally be driven to rage at his own recognition of the gulf between his real feelings and the role he played.

Now Joe was hurt, wounded, and in pain so great he could not ignore it. Depressed and guilt-ridden, he was forced, for the first time in his life, to take a good look at himself. He did not like what he saw.

Joe had always been a churchgoer. It went with his image. His Christianity, however, was a shallow facade. Now he felt that maybe there were values there that he had overlooked and that real success for him would be found in "authenticity." He was literally driven to centering prayer, where his being was more important than his activity. His false self became obvious even to him. He began to learn that activity sprang from being, and only if he learned to be loving could he act lovingly and be truly loved.

Joe had always wanted his marriage to be a success. He persuaded Marge to return and, this time, worked for an ideal marriage, not for the image but because he appreciated its real value as a sacrament and reflection of Christ's love for his church.

Low self-esteem had never been Joe's problem. In fact, he thought too much of himself. His defeats in marriage and politics hurt badly. He did not feel that he deserved either one of these wounds and spent a long time in the victim stage. In fact this was good for him. He also needed the anger stage in order to realize that he had to forgive his parents who had driven him to where he was and to himself whom he recognized as being chiefly responsible.

It was Marge who really become Joe's therapist. She knew him much better than he knew himself and could see through the images he was constantly projecting. She helped him look at his pain. She had watched him run from it for years and knew how harmful his emotional deprivation was for him.

When Joe realized that he had his wife's love even when he was not successful, he was able to breath a sigh of relief and relax. The barricades he had built around himself began to fall and he gradually began to admit his needs, re-establish his values, and put his winning abilities to genuine and valued purposes. He no longer had to live a life of deceit. He did not have to hide everything that did not fit the expected image.

Joe no longer looks at victory as the way to happiness but rather sees happiness as a victory. He still is a man of high energy and creative ideas and still is able to move others to develop their potential to achieve. It was only when he was able to admit his defeat and face his inadequacies that Joe was able truly to become a real winner.

Joe's woundedness had resulted in his repressing or under-valuing his own emotional needs and his relationships His freedom to love was wounded early in life. It was painful for Joe to realize his lack of love, both for himself or for others. Success was his distraction and his substitute for loving. He needed to forgive himself. Comforting the child within (see chapter 6) will help him, as will focusing (chapter 27). Even though he belongs to the heart center (the tin man), he is not in touch with it. His dreams, especially the ones that leave him with indeterminate feelings of anxiety, have much to tell him.

Joe needs to forgive those who pushed him to succeed, especially his father. To help himself realize that true success lies in accepting his own inadequacies as the first step toward loving, he would do well to spend some time meditating on certain scripture passages (see scriptural meditation in chapter 24), like the following: Psalm 62 (for his anxiety); Jn 3:17–21 (to face the truth); Lk 17:7–10 (for humble service over accomplishments). (For other useful Scripture texts, see *The Enneagram and Prayer* in the bibliography.)

17

Louise, the Romantic

There is a play in New York City called *The Fantasticks*. It has been running for forty years. It opens with a somewhat typical sixteen-year-old girl who soliloquizes on her specialness. After a while she pauses, looks vacantly into the middle distance, returns, and pleads, "Oh God, please don't let me be ordinary."

Louise Palermo can identify with this. Being special defines her very being. Louise has never married. She claims that she is married to her career, owning and operating a small but exquisite gift shop in a resort town on Cape Cod.

Louise learned early in life that she could not count on her parents for emotional support. Not physically but emotionally abandoned by wealthy parents with an extensive social life, her earliest memories are connected with a sense of deprivation and loss. She was raised by a series of maids and housekeepers and sent away to school as soon as it was feasible. She was often given promises of future vacations and prolonged trips and stays with her parents which, for the most part, never eventualized. Each disappointment resulted in a bout of depression, when Louise would fantasize and invent for herself a close, loving family where she was a center of love and care.

Louise, as she grew older, often vacillated between the anger and the self-blame stages. She experienced outrage at having been deprived of a normal family life and anger at the parents who were responsible. Her parents died when she was fifteen in an automobile accident, further establishing her feeling of abandonment. She directed her anger inwardly in the self-blame stage. She was simply not good enough to have been given the love and affection she craved.

Depression was a common feeling for Louise. Her better moods could probably be described as melancholy. A yearning for things that never were and probably would never be. In the sadness of her melancholy, Louise would isolate herself and allow images, fantasies and imaginative stories to fill her time and her mind. She developed a fondness, even a need, for communicating her moods through symbols and artistic expression.

Her pain and sense of loss placed her outside the common herd. She was unique and special and no one could possibly understand her. Her theme song became "Nobody knows the trouble I've seen, nobody knows my sorrow." She actually relished her wounds, embellished them, and would not stop their bleeding or permit their healing. The victim stage became her life. She was stuck in it. It became the source of her energy and the font of her artistic expression.

As a teenager the possibility of suicide fascinated her and she even envied a close friend who took her own life. She lived at the extremes of her emotional swings. Most of her emotions were either directed to the past or to the imaginary future scenarios of her lonesome reveries.

At one time Louise was engaged to a young policeman. She enjoyed his "presence" more when he was absent as her fantasies about him were far in excess of anything he could possibly live up to. He left her because he could not deal with her intensity. Wounded and abandoned again, Louise separated herself from her friends to cherish and lick her wounds. Nobody could console her because nobody could possibly know what her sorrows were like. Eventually she fantasized herself into a new (imaginary) relationship in the vague future when everything would be better.

Louise's self-esteem was low as is usual for victims. She also frequently visited the self-blame stage. If she had only been prettier, more intelligent, more lovable she would not have been abandoned by her parents. Strangely, Louise would compensate for her low self-esteem by adopting an elegant facade. She dressed uniquely but tastefully, knew how to wear make-up in a different but attractive fashion, and wore jewelry with taste and distinction. She would be different, unique, superior, and thought she would find love this way.

At her best, Louise was a warm friend and a compassionate listener who attracted a devout following. She was creative, supportive, refined, and interestingly different. At her worst she would be depressed, guilt-ridden, withdrawn, moody, and self-absorbed. If someone misunderstood her, she felt personally attacked and added another bleeding wound to her repertoire. She often wondered when her real life would begin. She was attracted to men who were unsuitable or unavailable and thus added to her hurts.

Louise needs to get out of the denial stage and admit that her childhood sense of loss was real and then set it aside to move on with her life. She is too easily captured and captivated by the ego absorption of the self-guilt and the victim stages. For her there did not seem to be much of a forward motion, more a constant vacillation from one stage to the other until she felt like a rubber band.

She needs to work constructively to supply for the abandonment and the lack of love and acceptance of her childhood by treating herself lovingly. A prayer life supported by scriptural mediations (see chapter 24) would help her to see her real value before God. Her ability at imaging could serve to make the gospel alive, real, and relevant to her as she prayerfully entered into the situations and events of the life of Jesus. Louise would have no trouble identifying with the woman at the well, the widow who gave her mite at the temple, or the Blessed Mother sorrowfully offering her son at the cross.

It is important for her not to look for further wounding by magnifying all out of proportion things others might say or do that she found offensive. Interpersonal issues like these should be deal with quickly and, insofar as possible, with controlled emotions. One of the tools useful for escaping the victim stage would be good for her, e.g., keeping a list of the things that she is thankful for and adding to it day by day. Her fantasy ideals and her active imagination are good things when they are not overdone and if they can, even only once in a while, be put into action. She must learn to live in the present.

Louise should work on her special ability to create beauty through her artistic leaning. She must recognize her shadow side with its large quota of unreasonable envy and learn to live in the real world, which will not be such a bad place after all. Beautiful people create a beautiful world. The focusing process described in chapter 27 could do wonders for her as she learns to recognize what her painful feelings are telling her. Centering meditation could be very important in getting her away from her personal preoccupation as it could be for each of the three types in the relational (heart) center.

18
Carl, the Thinker

Carl's favorite artistic work is Rodin's sculpture, *The Thinker*. It is a larger than life bronze of a naked man sitting with a far away or inward look on his face, his head gracefully resting on his bent wrist in an attitude of deep reflection. He is naked because he cannot be bothered with the trappings of social convention and involvement while he fathoms the meaning of reality.

Carl knows nothing about his biological parents. He was adopted when two years old by a couple who were trying him out as a way to save their marriage. They never divorced but merely tolerated each other until they died within a two-year period when Carl was fifty. It was only after their deaths that he realized the ambiguity of his feelings for them. He loved them for the care and nurturing he had received. They were never really cruel or abusive. But he hated them for the obsessive ways in which they interfered in his life, even as a child. He was the only thing his parents had in common, and they both took an interest in the details of his life, seldom leaving him an opportunity for privacy.

Aware of his adoption from his earliest childhood, Carl sensed that his parents used this as a coercive measure to make him pliant to their intrusions. Carl shut off his emotions as a way of escape. He was not usually allowed to stay in his room, having to study and play under his mother's eye constantly. He learned to build his own walls in a desperate effort for some privacy. One of his favorite fantasies as a child was to become invisible.

There was no lion (gut center) in Carl's life. He withdrew to the intellectual reveries of the scarecrow (mind center). He saw everything, even his emotions, as objects of intellectual speculation. His few childhood friends were bonded mostly by their mutual interest in collecting stamps. In school he responded well to the overemphasis on the intellectual center (scarecrow) to the detriment especially of the body center (lion). Carl was wounded in the very heart of his being. His inner emptiness was frightening. He thought that he had no emotional problems because he kept them under control and was proficient in analyzing them. He seldom actually felt them. Most of his life was spent in the denial stage, and he was not even aware of that. The denial stage is very strong in Carl's life, but it is also very subtle. He thinks that he knows his wounds and he probably does, but that is precisely his problem. He knows them but refuses to feel them, at least on a conscious level. They are neatly compartmentalized in his intellectual center. He needs to feel his victimization and its subsequent energizing anger. He needs passion in his life in order to grow. The pain of unhealed wounds when faced emotionally can help him.

In college, because of the influence of a much-admired professor, he majored in English literature and thought he would like to teach it on a high school level. Not feeling sufficiently prepared with a bachelor's degree, he went on for his master's. At this point, he realized that he would never be ready to teach and got a job, successfully maintained, as a computer analyst for marketing. He liked this work which was solitary and where he was, for the most part, free from supervision.

Information to Carl was like gold to a miser, collected for its own sake and not for what it could contribute to society. He was a fringe person, always observing, never participating.

His wounded emptiness hardened around him like a shell so that neither he nor anyone else could penetrate it. As he later came to acknowledge, he married Sylvia because she "respected his need for privacy" and acted as a buffer to reduce outside interference. His children quickly were taught that his den was his castle and even though he was a good family man, his privacy there in his den was to be kept inviolate. He continued his stamp collection and became an insatiable Civil War buff.

Carl needs to experience the anger stage. He surpresses anger because it is too frightening for him and pretends to deal with it by analyzing. He needs it directed outside of himself and as a force impelling him to action rather than analysis.

Carl has a natural attraction towards meditation. Centering prayer (see chapater 26) would help him to let go of the chatter of his intellectualizations and find his true inner reality, the love which is God. This, in turn, will manifest itself in his daily life as he begins to live the contemplative attitude. He needs to recognize that he is a loving and beloved man.

The compassion meditation (see chapter 25) is important for Carl. He needs and probably even wants to forgive his parents. He must experience his feelings towards them. It is not too late for him to deal with them even though they are dead.

Discursive meditation, reflection with and on the Scriptures, also involving some very personal conversations with Jesus or with the Blessed Virgin, will help him to get in touch with himself and enable him to realize and release some of his deep feelings without fear or threat. Wisdom in its deepest form is a blending of knowing, willing, and feeling into an integral whole. Prayer, relating deliberately to the Source of all wisdom, to Wisdom Incarnate, can do this for Carl.

Perhaps this is the only way he will begin to confront the wound of his shadow issue of miserliness. First, he will recognize that it exists, then, he will realize that knowledge acquired is not merely for personal use but for sharing. He will also be led to humility, to accept his limitations and not be afraid to share his partial knowledge because he will no longer see others reactions as a substitute for his own feelings but will truly desire to share with them what he does have. In this way he will come full circle. His sharing will be responded to; his knowledge will be increased by the others' responses. He will appreciate the adage: The way to learn is to become a teacher. This will be the fruit of his wholeness and forgiveness for his early wounds and, indeed for all of the hurts he suffered but ignored throughout his life.

The advantage of being a thinker can now be used to its fullest. His ability to stand back and view life objectively will not be motivated by fear but by a healthy desire to learn. He will examine the structure of things, learning causes and effects in order to put this knowledge to useful purposes. His sense of integrity will be maintained, doing what he knows to be correct instead of bowing to social conventions. He will still be attracted to and need privacy but will be able, when called upon, to respond to social situations. Moving towards action will be for him a way of getting in touch with his body (the lion—his repressed center). He will use his anger as a power to energize and motivate rather than a wounding and implosive force to withdraw. He will experience life more broadly and increase his knowledge to share it further.

The focusing process would be much to his advantage because it would help him to be aware of his hurts. He would probably find it difficult at first, but very worthwhile when he gets the hang of it.

A personal relationship with God such as is encountered in a prayer group where some moderate emotional expression is encouraged would be good for Carl even though he would find it difficult. To forgive on a feeling level, Carl needs to break through his intellectual miserliness. Generosity and willingness to share his gifts can be encouraged by meditating on 1Tm 6:17–19 and Mt 25:31–46.

19
Ben, the Coordinator

If you were to ask Ben to describe himself, he would probably respond with something like: "I am a loyal person but also a very cautious one." Ben has been in middle management for years. He is the director of a department in a New York City garment factory. Fifty people, mostly women and mostly immigrants, work under him. Ben has managed to keep a balanced middle ground in responding to the demands of the company and the needs of the workers he supervises.

He sees in his job a pattern he followed in the army. There he was also in middle management as a master sergeant who had to mediate the demands of his superior officers with the responses and needs of the men he commanded. He had considered making military life a career. He liked the disciplined and orderly life but was too uneasy with the suspicions and the distrust he felt with ambitious professionals who, he said, used him as a stepping stone to further their own careers. What Ben described as cautious, others saw as overly suspicious.

Ben has spent many weekends attending workshops on communication skills and management strategies. He is an anxious person, but rather than confront his anxieties, he tends to project them, through his suspicions, onto others. At times he feels paranoid and is sure that both his bosses and his workers are out to get him.

Ben deals with his wife and three children in much the same way he deals with his job-related personnel. Togetherness, loyalty, group action, and duty are what he teaches his children both by word and example. When he got married, he changed his religion for the sake of his wife and, while he is loyal to his new commitments, he has frequent guilt feelings in relation to his former beliefs.

Addicted to security, Ben fears risks of any kind. Preoccupied by all the dangerous possibilities that could interfere with his family or his job, his anxieties cause him at times to overplan and to procrastinate. He can easily identify with the insecurity of his workers but, at the same time, tends to be on the lookout constantly for threats, often imaginary, coming from them.

An abiding sense of fear is a constant companion in Ben's life. He lacks self-confidence which causes him not only to distrust others (by projecting his own suspicions) but also to overconsult and hence to delay action.

On the other hand, Ben's need for security and his tendency to project prompts him towards a real concern for others—for their comfort and security. One result of this is that Ben is an excellent host, very considerate of his guests and anxious for their comfort and ease.

Ben (and others like him) tends to repress the intellectual center (the scarecrow). He does not trust the perspective gained by looking at the big picture. He does consult others a lot (often too much) but does not place a lot of confidence in their opinions. His life wound extends back to his childhood. His brother, two years older, was a Downs Syndrome child, and Ben was raised with a sense of duty and responsibility for him. His parents often placed more burdens on him regarding care for his brother than he was able to carry. As a result, his freedom to trust, both himself and others, was wounded. A sense of insecurity resulted from not knowing where he stood in his parents' love. Even as an adult Ben can never obtain sufficient affirmations to carry him through his duties. Even when he is given support and backing for one job, the next day he starts out again alone and suspicious. He needs to develop his intellectual center so he can realize a balance between his inner and outer worlds. His wounded ability to trust is expressed in his ongoing need for reassurance. Because he does not trust, he lives in an untrusting world. Many of Ben's wounds are self-inflicted, rising from his own suspicions and doubts, which are projected on others around him.

Centering prayer can be important for Ben. By putting aside his ego or false self, he can learn to trust in God and find his reassurances in love. He does not need so much to be told this in theory but to experience it in practice. Also by comforting the child within, as described earlier, he can get in touch with his heart center and help make up for the lack of love responsible for his wounds. Scriptural meditation on God's love, on placing confidence in God's will, and on placing his life on trust in God's hands are important and maturing for him. Because of his underlying fear of life, he needs to consider Jesus' teaching in Mt 10:26–33. He wants and needs the guidance and strength of the Holy Spirit, as is promised in Jn 16:13–16.

20
Peter, the Optimist

Peter is appropriately named because his type of personality is often called the Peter Pan Type. He carries the image of eternal youth. The burdens and cares of age weigh lightly on his shoulders, and the only wrinkles ever on his face will be laugh lines. An African American, born and raised in Roxbury, Massachusetts, in what was once an Irish ghetto but which in Peter's lifetime was always an enclosure for various non-Caucasian races, Peter has been accused, and justly so, by his peers as lacking any vestige of black rage. In fact, he can never really understand or feel "what the fuss is all about." This, in spite of the fact that he lived through some of the most important and tumultuous years of African-American liberation from Selma to Los Angeles.

Peter's father and two of his older brothers served jail sentences for civil protest, drug dealing, and armed burglary respectively. If asked to describe his childhood in one word, Peter would reply, "It was very happy" and try to believe it was, in spite of the facts. Police raids, ghetto riots, and drug traffic were a part of his preschool and school years. His only escape in his early years was by way of his imagination. There he lived in a Disney world of his own making, far removed from the frightening realities of everyday ghetto life. For the rest of his life, Peter will cover over his early fears with visionary plans backed up by many options to provide for possible failures.

He avoids alcohol and drugs, having seen what they did and are doing to so many of his family and friends. He claims to have no need of such stimulants because he is "high on life." He was too young to be an active participant in the flower-child culture of the 1960s but he looks to it for inspiration and still believes in the fantasized images of society painted by hippie imagination. He finds meaning in their slogans such as: "Make love not war" or "Today is the first day of the rest of your life."

Peter is the only one of his family to graduate from college and has, by way of his pleasant, optimistic personality and active imagination, worked himself up to an executive position in a public relations firm. He had tried brief careers in teaching, social work, and short-order cooking

His financial position and social status now allow him to seek and possess many of the long-coveted elements of the "good life," but he often finds enjoyment on the wane, giving way to obscure feelings of insecurity and anxiety. This leads him to further pursue his pleasures even to the point of whirling hyperactivity which usually leads to even more anxiety. The pull of anxiety, which wants to draw him into himself, is a fearful undertow which he responds to by excessive extroversion.

At one time he was into a museum "kick," spending much time visiting the special showings abounding in the Boston area. He gave this up for the music of night clubs and bar-hopping even though he seldom drank. Then on to something else, never realizing that as long as he oriented himself to externals, the real Peter could never be a part of his activities. He became like the frightened quarry of Francis Thompson's "Hound of Heaven," always fleeing, hiding, turning to one amusement after another and always with a sense that there was something (or Someone!) pursuing him through the persistent proddings of his anxiety.

Peter thinks that for him forgiveness is not only easy, it isn't even necessary. He brushes off the traumas of the white domination of his childhood and the continual injustices of the predominant white culture of his present life. His constant desire for instant gratification makes anything like a long-term process of forgiveness unthinkable on any serious level even though, in his better moments, he anxiously senses a need for it in his life.

When frustrated, Peter easily becomes angry, even enraged. He controls it by external distractions, seldom looking within himself to try to discover the unconscious motivations behind his wrath. On the whole, though, especially as he matures, Peter is fun to be with, energetic, a great story teller, imaginative, invigorating, and always able to bounce up from disappointments.

It is obvious by now that Peter tends to live in the denial stage. If he is to forgive, and he has much to forgive especially regarding people, circumstances, and institutions from his early life, he must first acknowledge his wounds. An honest facing of perplexing and conflicting emotions by way of the focusing process (see chapter 27) will be especially helpful. Peter would find it easy to enter into Gospel passages in a combined focusing and scriptural type of prayer. Maybe he could try to be St. Peter in Mk 8:31 ff. and experience the seriousness of Jesus' stern prediction of the future, or rejoice in the optimism of Col 3:1–7 and the hope that forgiveness brings. Peter needs also to forgive himself and even allow God to minister to him as when Jesus washes St. Peter's feet in Jn 13:1–16.

Peter's weakest center of knowledge is relational (the heart center). Acknowledging hurts, even trivial ones, and consciously (even if only to himself) forgiving the perpetrators will make him more aware of his own offenses.

Like his two previous companions in the brain center (scarecrows), Peter needs to get away from his ongoing intellectualizations and planning through the wordless love of centering prayer. He will have to be aware, however, of his attraction to altered states of consciousness as a way of escape. At the same time, because his weakest center is relational (heart—tin man), he should frequently look about himself to see the needs of others and to face them in intercessory prayer.

21
Esther, the Champion

Esther was raised in an Orthodox Jewish family in South Africa. She recalls her childhood as a time of overbearing domination by a mother determined to shape her into the mold proper to nice Jewish girls. From her earliest years, she fought these attempts, not only from her mother but from her teachers and the all-pervasive religious culture surrounding her. She refused her family's efforts to direct her into a teaching career or an early life of domestic routine. When she was twenty-five she emigrated to Israel. There she found the support she wanted to pursue an independent life and entered the Law School of Hebrew University. Shortly after graduation she married another Israeli lawyer and settled down to a profitable but humdrum routine of practicing law and raising two sons and a daughter according to Orthodox expectations.

As a lawyer Esther was attracted to the defense of the weak. She took great pride in being their champion. Usually she saw the cases she dealt with in terms of right or wrong, black or white, and polarized the victimizers as brutal tyrants who had to feel the full thrust of her strong defense for the victims of their injustices. She got energy from opposition and literally knew no fear either from individuals, corporations, the government, or the legal system.

It was not long before the legal and civil injustices perpetrated by the Israeli government on Palestinian Arabs caught her attention. Outraged by the rampant and obvious injustices she witnessed, she turned her legal expertise to defending Palestinians and challenging manifestly illegal activities of government agencies in depriving Palestinians of their homes, their job opportunities, and their civil freedom. Eventually she accepted a full-time job defending Palestinian victims of Israeli government abuses offered to her by a United Nations agency. Esther was not at all dismayed that she was now fighting her friends, her country, her religious inculturations, and even her family. At least that is what she told herself. In reality the tender, sensitive little girl very much alive within her and the very reason she was so eager to defend the weak, was greatly affected, hurt, and vulnerable. Her unconscious reaction to this was to enter all the more vigorously into her professional commitments to fight the government abuses. Eventually disgusted by what she saw as Israeli–Jewish persecution of a minority in their own backyard, Esther did the unthinkable: She became a Christian. Her husband and three teenage children left her, and she waded into the morass of social, legal, and religious disapproval and opposition. Labeled by former friends as a "self-hating Jew," she literally took on her world, as she knew it.

In self-defense Esther had lived out her life without really looking into herself or being conscious of the vulnerable and delicate child she carried within her. Always she looked outside herself to discover who was to blame. Now her abandonment actually forced her to severe, painful introversion and examination of feelings and real motivations. She began to recognize her need to control the world around her, her space, her time, her possessions, and the significant people in her life. Aided by her newfound religion and new sympathetic friends, she was led to moderate her instant denial of the validity of other people's opposing points of view and her all-or-nothing way of seeing things in extremes.

Even while she deplored the injustices her work forced her to face, she was challenged by the issues and the people she had to defend. She lost the sense of boredom she had felt as a part-time housewife and directed the energy once expended on secondary or insignificant "middle-class issues" to injustices attracting national and even international attention.

Esther eventually sought and recovered an uneasy but loving relationship with her family—but never their full approval. She realized then that their abandonment had hurt her far more than she was willing to admit. She felt, however, that they now respected her strength even though they could not support her goals. She still tends however to debunk their disapproval and tries to make light of their objections.

If she admitted to wounds at all, Esther saw them only as places of scars which were stronger than the original tissue— something which energized her and enabled her to fight more vigorously than ever. Now that her mother is elderly and in need of support, care, and affirmation, Esther finds it easy to respond to her but is still wary of getting too close. Her denial stage, still very prominent, is limited mostly to an unconscious refusal to admit self-inflicted wounds. Esther needs, most of all, to forgive herself.

Esther needs to learn how to be vulnerable. She is vulnerable in the sensitive girl who lives within her, but her whole approach to life is one of hiding or denying this. When she is wounded, she hits back with swift and brutal blows. The principles of nonviolence as taught by Ghandi or Martin Luther King, Jr., as they deal with attitudes as well as actions, are very useful for her, especially as she does find them attractive in a paradoxical way.

Scriptural meditation on the fatherhood (motherhood) of God will help her to focus on her own dependencies. God's tenderness and Jesus' ability to compassionate with both sides of an issue can be, for her, valuable tools. The realization that she is responsible for much of her own woundedness could hit Esther with devastating force. To counteract her negative or shadow issue, she would find some of the following texts helpful: on excessive desire for power, Lk 22:24–27; on reluctance to admit weaknesses, 2Co 12:7–10; on over self-reliance, Eph 2:1–10. To reinforce her strengths and emphasize her giftedness, she would profit by the following: 2Co 6:3–10 on willingness to pay the price for doing God's work; her concern for the weak is supported by Is 61:1–9; Mt 11:28–30 will support her honest attempt to face her weaknesses and find support in Jesus.

Esther tends to deny painful wounds that she does not want to face by diverting her attention, often to pleasurable excesses. She needs to recognize the denial stage. Scriptural meditation will greatly facilitate the kind of self-examination she tends to avoid.

The practice of centering prayer will allow her to face her vulnerability, to rest in God's love, and to be energized by grace rather than by defensive reactions to personal fear of vulnerability. She would also learn much about herself by claiming the feelings aroused in herself by those qualities in opponents she finds most unappealing. To focus on these feelings according to the method described in chapter 27 would be very revealing. The compassion meditation would be valuable for her because her weakest center is the relational one (heart). She needs the experience of compassionate responses and attitudes toward opponents (enemies!).

22
Robert, the Pacifier

Robert has held the same job since his graduation from high school twenty-five years ago. He started as a shipping clerk for a large shoe manufacturing company. After several promotions he now holds a fairly good position in personnel, for the most part interviewing job applicants. He works hard in mostly routine matters and has a certain appeal for apprehensive job applicants due to his nonthreatening appearance and attitude. Robert claims he is very much aware of the "Peter Principle" and is avoiding its outcome—which is to be promoted to a level where he would be incompetent. He insists that he is happy to stay right where he is until his eagerly-looked-for retirement in fifteen more years when he claims that he will be intricately involved in "doing nothing."

His wife and two grown sons would describe him as "laid back." His friends appreciate his sense of humor and his noncritical acceptance of their own good and bad points. What they don't realize is that, while he has lots of friends, he really has no close friends. For him it is "out of sight, out of mind." When someone is present to him, he is entirely theirs. Seemingly attentive (but not really!), he gives himself to them even to the point of identifying or blending with their personality or point of view. However, when they are absent, he seems to have little concern or interest in them. Seldom does he take the initiative to reach out to someone or to initiate some mutual activity. The way he justifies it to himself is, "I don't want to bother anybody." What he is really saying is, "I don't want to bother myself."

Robert can be very energetic when it is really needed and when he is highly motivated. Yet his shadow side is sloth. In fact, Robert, as his wife will tell you, is a couch potato. Most of his free time is spent narcotized before a TV set. He is great at postponing things. "Why do it today when, if you wait until tomorrow, it may not be necessary to do it at all." Robert has to motivate himself daily to get up in the morning. "After all," he says, "you do have to have a reason to get out of bed."

Since his early childhood, when he learned that the best way to survive is to steer clear of trouble and blend into the background, he has pursued an unremitting goal to avoid conflict. This is both his virtue and his vice. He will run from, ignore, or deny conflictual situations. Yet, at the same time, he is a good peacemaker, generally refusing to take sides, able to listen to all points of view, and always looking for some kind of harmonious consensus. This is perhaps what his two sons remember best from their childhood and their frequent boyhood squabbles, and it may be his greatest gift to them.

Robert would say that forgiveness is not an issue with him because "there is nothing to forgive." This is really an unfortunate rationalization. Forgiveness means that a wound (a conflict!) has been inflicted, and he is reluctant to face such conflicts in his life. It is much easier for him to deny them. So he lives much of his life in one form or other of the denial stage. He has some significant childhood issues which can only be truly resolved by first admitting them and then forgiving the persons or institutions responsible. For one thing, he has a forgiveness issue to deal with regarding his mother. He feels she never listened to him and that his point of view was always ignored in favor of one or other of his siblings. He feels this is still true.

Although he would like to deny it, Robert has a deep abiding cauldron of anger seething below the surface. Having seen what he is like when it erupts, he is even afraid of it himself. One of the things that can bring this anger out is pressure. Robert hates pressure and deadlines. Instead of instigating him to activity, these things paralyze him. Sometimes they make him feel victimized and taken advantage of. The anger that arises then can, if used properly, serve to energize him, or it can be directed at innocent others in an irrational outburst. It is important for him to be able to step aside to recognize his woundedness. He must be willing to admit, face, and be compassionate about the conflictual elements and people in his life.

Centering prayer could be very appealing, simple, and helpful to him. He has a natural ability to blend or meld with others, especially loved ones. This is really the process of centering directed towards God.

The emotions that arise and are indirectly noticed when he goes off on one of his frequent mental tangents to avoid facing a possible conflictual situation should be embraced and heard as useful teachers. He can do this through the focusing process. He has to develop a sensitivity to these feelings and learn to listen to their healing possibilities and to allow them to perform their function of leading him from denial to healing.

For scriptural meditation, Rev 3:14–16 would help Robert realize that constant tepidity is not a Christian lifestyle. Because he can be offended by the intrinsic demands placed on him by authorities, society, and religion, or he could be helped by meditating on Mt 25:14–30 and the use of his God-given talents.

He needs to give some real attention to the anger stage. When he feels anger, he is feeling wounded. He must relate this source of energy to the healing process.

23

Mildred, the Perfectionist

Mildred conforms, in many ways, to the typical stereo-
type of the fourth-grade teacher. Prim and proper, she is to be
seen standing before her thirty pupils at Washington Gram-
mar School in Denver "shoulding on them." Moral issues,
social conduct, proper behavior—all the things they "should"
do—are very important to Mildred. Indeed this was a major
factor in her decision to become a teacher. Her home is like
her classroom. Everything is in its place, and she exercises an
unrelenting vigilance on the proper conduct of her three girls,
her husband, and, above all, on herself.

Early in life Mildred learned that the best way to be
accepted, approved, and loved was to fulfill the expectations
of significant others. She still carries vividly in her memory
the picture of her mother shaking her finger at her saying,
"Now, Mildred, good little girls always. . . ." Mildred has spent
the rest of her life filling in that sentence and following it. In
fact, she carries in her mind a little voice very similar to that of
her mother, constantly criticizing everything, her environment, her friends, her family, and herself.

Her criticism is automatic and unceasing. Even when she
does not consciously realize it, her mind is running amok criticizing and correcting everything she sees. It is an exhausting

practice and takes much of her energy. At the same time, it pushes her into the activity needed to correct things.

Mildred is hard working. She has to be because it is her goal in life to make everything perfect. That indeed is hard work, and she sets to it vigorously. Her problem is that she has an impossible task. As a result she is always angry—angry at the imperfections of the world, at the deficiencies of the school system in which she works, at the inadequacies of her children, the social system, and the sloppiness of her husband in not washing the sink after shaving.

Perhaps the most difficult thing for Mildred, and often something she is not even conscious of, is that she is not allowed to express that anger. To express anger is imperfect so she cannot allow herself to indulge in it. She can be angry, however, when it is socially acceptable. Then she goes at it with a vengeance, such as the time she suspected that one of her fourth-grade boys was a battered child. Investigation proved that she was correct and, since that time, she has carried on a public campaign of outrageous opposition, anger-inspired and expressing support for any organization supporting battered children or women. In this way, she channels much of her anger and externalizes it in a positive manner.

Other things are not so simple for Mildred, but as she learns to observe herself and her activities with a certain amount of objectiveness, she experiences the expansion and freedom that comes with a balanced maturity. A significant step for her, for example, came at a PTA meeting when she was pursuing her ideas for a fund-raising for an art project. Suddenly she noticed that, while her suggestion was a good one, there were half a dozen others that could be of equal value. One of her life maxims came crashing down—her mother's dictum, "Mildred there is only one right way to do a thing," fell on its face, and Mildred realized with a flood of relief and insight that there were actually dozens of right ways to do this fund-raising and, indeed, to do most other things in life. This has helped her to realize that the world is really shades of gray and not black and white and, even more importantly, to realize that this is all right.

Mildred does not think she has any problems with forgiveness. After all, it is the proper thing to do, and she always does the proper thing. She honestly can't think of a single person or incident that she has not forgiven, including an episode of sexual abuse perpetrated by an uncle when she was six years old. What she does not realize, however, is that much of her "forgiving" is shallow, merely a form and only on the intellectual level. She forces herself to forgive because that is the right thing to do, but deep down the wounds are still there, painful and unhealed.

Mildred has to forgive herself, others, and the world for not being perfect. Her anger can be very useful for this if she can get in touch with it. She has to be aware of the indirect ways she externalizes it. Then she can bring it to consciousness. The set of her shoulders, a firm pursing of the lips, or an overreaction of excessive politeness are clues that anger is present and suppressed. The focusing process (see chapter 27) will help examine that anger and what it is telling her of wholeness.

Mildred would be attracted to centering prayer even if, at times, she found it difficult. After all, isn't loving God the most "perfect" form of prayer? In this area, at least, her perfectionism may serve her in good stead. She would not be overly concerned with putting aside intellectual activity and control, as her primary center of understanding is instinctual (gut center—the lion). It is important for her also to understand and accept the value of vulnerability as a preventative to receiving wounds or, at least, as a reaction to hurts.

For scriptural meditation it would be good for Mildred to consider the place of the weeds among the wheat as expressed in Mt 13:24–30. Using the same type of metaphor, she could profit by relaxing in God's providence and letting him run his world as in Mk 4:26–27. Her tendency towards being judgmental could be tempered by praying over Mt 7:1–5. Also the compassion meditation would help Mildred to accept the weaknesses as well as the strong points of others and not to try to straitjacket them in her own standards of morality (perfection).

PART THREE

Tools for Forgiveness

The "tools" (processes and prayers) found in this section are all related to one another and have specific helpful roles in the forgiveness process. They are all oriented towards integral, spiritual wholeness of which forgiveness is a by-product. Their individual value for specific personality types has been indicated in the previous section. They are not to be limited, however, to personality types because each of us shares in the characteristics of each type and can profit from each of the tools.

The relationship of the tools to each other is signified by the order in which they are presented. Scripture meditation is first. It is concerned with revealing to us the truths about ourselves, our activity, and our motivations. It is also concerned with revealing to us the truths about a loving God.

To know ourselves and to know God with the aid of God's revelation in Scripture inclines us to a compassionate (God-like) unconditional love. We express this in the compassion meditation in dealing with our neighbor and in the centering meditation in dealing with God. A not-infrequent product of both these meditations are unclear but very real feelings that may arise during centering or be triggered by the compassion meditation. Focusing on these feelings according to the focusing process will bring us to the healing our body knowledge (our gut, or lion center) offers us through these feelings. Finally vulnerability will render us docile to the loving promptings of the Spirit and place us in an habitual loving attitude, not prone to receive even painful attacks from others as personal wounds.

24
Scriptural Meditation

The phrase we monks use for spiritual reading is *lectio divina*. Literally, it means divine reading, but it involves a great deal more than mere reading.

The process of *lectio* is a simple one. It is a form of prayer which can and should embrace every level of prayer. The book used for *lectio*, whatever it may be, is chosen as a means of hearing the Lord speak in human words. This, of course, means that the Bible is the *lectio* book par excellence. Yet any book with a general spiritual orientation is actually nothing other than a commentary on the Bible, and so is quite acceptable for *lectio*.

There are four levels of mental activity: information—a gathering of facts, knowledge—a classifying of those facts; understanding—an experience which those facts represent; and wisdom—a relating of that information, knowledge, and understanding to our ultimate goal, which is God. The reading of *lectio divina* is oriented towards wisdom. In it we attempt to see the facts of our lives, our value systems, and our experiences precisely as they relate to and further our part in the building up of God's kingdom. We also open ourselves, in the books we read, to the experiences of others and to their particular wisdom, and seek to apply it in our own lives.

The most important element in *lectio divina*, however, is openness to the inspiration of the Holy Spirit. We give the Spirit the opportunity to speak to us through the Bible and through significant spiritual literature. This is a time given over precisely for this purpose alone. It is not seen as an opportunity to study (to gain information and knowledge), or to reflect specifically on our past (to gain understanding), but mostly to open our hearts and minds to the suggestions of the Holy Spirit as a result of our reading (this is wisdom).

We do not open a book in *lectio divina* in order to finish it, but in order to hear what it is saying to us. Thus we read slowly, carefully, and attentively, often stopping to reflect on the meaning. Sometimes we read only one page in an hour, sometimes many. When we feel the grace to do so, we stop and pray according to the inspirations we may receive. I have often spent six months or more on one particular book selected for *lectio*, and have reread particularly inspiring books several times.

Let me share something which I learned in my own experience of *lectio divina* and prayer. It stems from our understanding of the Church's teaching on inspiration. The Scriptures are inspired. Traditionally this word has had two meanings. In the first centuries of Christianity, the dominant meaning was that when the Scriptures were read and listened to, God spoke through them directly to the assembly or the individual.

Another meaning for inspiration has also been more or less prominent at different times in the history of the Church. It had to do with the authors of the various books in the Scriptures. Inspiration here meant that the Holy Spirit was in some way present to the author when he wrote his particular part of the Bible. Thus what was written was under the inspiration of the Holy Spirit and must be considered as the word of God. Much of the theological speculation regarding this notion of inspiration had to do with the manner in which the Spirit influenced the writer. Did the Spirit actually dictate the words? Did the Spirit influence the style of the author, or let him use his own personality to express divine truths? Was the author used mechanically, as we would use a pen or a computer, or did he have more or less complete freedom of expression, simply being guided by the Spirit so that he would not teach error?

It was Martin Luther who restored to the Church the important and practical understanding of inspiration. This aspect refers to the presence of the Holy Spirit in the word of God inspiring the listeners to believe, understand, and take to heart the wisdom of God, expressed in the Bible, especially when it is read in the assembly of God's people. This meaning of inspiration has never been totally absent. It is readily demonstrated through our liturgical practices.

Note carefully what happens at Mass when the Gospel is about to be read. The priest or deacon stands at the lectern and personally greets the people: "The Lord be with you." The people respond to them and to the greeting: "And also with you." But then something incredible happens. The priest announces: "A reading from the Holy Gospel according to St. Mark," and then he disappears. He, the minister, is no longer present. The congregation simply ignores him as it now responds to the Lord who speaks his own word. The people reply: "Glory be to you, O Lord!" God is present and speaking as the Gospel is read. The people acknowledge this again at the end by addressing, not the priest, but Christ: "Praise be to you, Lord Jesus Christ!"

The presence of God in the Scriptures when they are read is a real presence. It is as real as the presence of God in heaven, in the assembly gathered in his name, in the sacraments, or in the Eucharist. They are all different modalities of God's presence but they are all real.

This is one of the ways in which Jesus fulfills his extraordinary promise to be with us always, to the end of the world.

It is also a fulfillment of his promise to send us the Holy Spirit to remind us of all the truths which he has taught us. This does not refer simply to a repetition of doctrines or divine principles as though they were things we had forgotten. It refers to inspiration—a breathing forth of the Holy Spirit that allows us to recognize the application of Jesus' teachings in our lives, how we should live them, understand them, and apply them to the concrete situations of our daily existence—once again, wisdom.

It is not necessary for us to await the gathering of the liturgical assembly to hear the Lord speak and to experience his inspiration. We can do this whenever we open the Scriptures in faith. Here are some suggested steps for an effective use of the Scriptures in *lectio divina*:

1. Build a church. Create for yourself a special environment in which you will recognize that you are doing something different, something special, something that will bring you into God's presence. This can be done by going into your bedroom, closing the door, and lighting a candle. It can be done simply by kneeling down in a private place, offering a brief prayer to be attentive to God's word, and then kissing the Bible and sitting down to listen.

2. Be aware that God has already spoken. You could not even begin this prayerful reading if God had not first summoned you to it by his grace. "No one can say Jesus is Lord unless he be given the power by the Holy Spirit" (1Co 12:3). You are already into your prayer. God has called you and you have answered by going apart, taking your Bible, and starting your prayer. Now it is God's turn.

3. Allow God now to speak through his Scriptures. Open the Bible, for example, to the Psalms or the Gospels. Read, listen to what God says for a verse or two until you wish to stop, and respond. God is speaking to you.

4. Prayer is a dialogue. Speak to God. Ask God for an understanding of the text. Ask how it applies to you. Listen again to what God says in your heart, the scriptural texts, or both, and respond again as you would in any conversation.

5. Decide beforehand how long you want to pray. Maybe ten or fifteen minutes is enough. When your time is up, thank God for God's presence and wisdom. Be prepared, when you can, to extend the conversation if you feel so inclined.

Prayer is a dialogue. It involves a give-and-take, a listening and a speaking. God speaks to us, we listen. We speak, God listens to us. It is really as simple as that. We must, however, realize that what God says to us is of extreme importance. We must give God the opportunity to speak and we must give ourselves the opportunity to listen.

Jesus is the Word. He is the Father's response (dialogue) to all of our needs. Through him the Father is always speaking in human accents the very fullness of what God is. God is saying everything from the *fiat* of creation to the bestowing of grace in all of its forms on humanity to the very final Amen which announces the complete fullness of the kingdom:

> In the beginning was the Word, and the Word was with God, and the Word was God. He was with God in the beginning. Through him all things were made; without him nothing was made that has been made. In him was life, and that life was the light of men. (Jn 1:1–4)

Because God is Father, he is personal. His word is addressed to every single individual in a personal way, responding to every need in every situation. Do we need to praise God? Do we need comfort? Do we need to be rebuked, loved, reassured, chastised, instructed, pacified? God always speaks the word that we need to hear (not always what we want to hear).

Using the Scriptures is an important helpful way to listen to God and hear just what God is saying to us. I like very much the questions in the front of the Gideon Bibles found in most motels, questions like: Are you sad? Read such and such a text. Are you happy? Are you guilty? Are you mourning? Are you confused? Read such and such a text. This is just what I am saying. God is already speaking the word which responds to your sorrow, pain, joy, confusion. Through the inspiration of the Scriptures, you need simply open the Bible to the text where God speaks to your problem or your present joys and listen.

This is what we do in *lectio divina*, when we enter into a dialogue with the Lord. All we have to do is to select a Scripture passage. It can actually be any one at all. Some people like to open the Bible at random. Others prefer to select some verses with which they are familiar, or the special verses referred to in part two in reference to the different personality types and what their needs are to facilitate for them the forgiveness process.

25

Compassion Meditation

The title of this chapter is carefully chosen. It is not concerned with meditation or compassion but with a meditation which is itself compassion. The origins of compassion meditation are found in Tibetan monasticism. I have freely made whatever adaptations seemed useful. It is a meditation that is easily learned and easily taught.

It is important to understand the use of the word *compassion*. It is intended as a substitute for the words *agape* (too foreign), *charity* (which has lost its meaning entirely), and *love* (much too ambiguous). Compassion grasps the essential meaning behind these words with its thrust of "suffering or feeling together with" found in its etymology. It is a relational word that is unifying and active.

Since the time of Christ, we Christians have been told that love (compassion) must be our identifying characteristic. We have no trouble in accepting this as an idea. Practicing it is quite something else. One of the major problems in living out this great commandment is that compassion is both an emotion and an act of the will. Thus our difficulties in truly loving (being compassionate) are explained away by saying that we must do it (act of the will) even though we do not feel it (emotion). We express this by a number of half truths and half rationalizations, such as: "I love her but I don't like her," or "We have a love-hate relationship," and even the coldly unsatisfying, "We must act as if we love one another, no matter how we feel."

Our traditional Christian spirituality does not really deal with the emotion of compassion. The reasons are manifold, not the least of which are traditional suspicions concerning the emotions stemming from our Platonian–Augustinian background. We have much to learn from traditions that have been free from such hang-ups. Compassion meditation is an attempt, which many have found useful, to blend the act of compassion (the will) with the feeling of compassion (the emotion).

There are three simple steps. In the first step, we choose a person from whom we have received love, charity, *agape*, compassion. It may be someone very much involved with our present lives, someone from the past, living or dead, a parent, relative, friend, or child. This first step does show us how important it is to be loved in order to love. If it should be too difficult for a given individual to select a clear and obvious person for whom love is felt, then it is not out of place to choose, God the Father/Mother, Jesus, or Mary. The important thing is that we choose someone for whom our love is an emotion, that is, for whom compassion is felt as well as being an act of the will.

Then to continue the first step, we simply allow ourselves to revel in this emotion. We receive it, we relish it, we remember it, and allow it to wash over us, to penetrate into our hearts and souls. And then we return it. We do this by directing our thoughts and feelings to this person in a loving compassionate way. We wish him/her peace, joy, healing, life, success, contentment, fulfillment. It is important to remember that these sentiments can be wished for someone who is "dead" as well as for the living. We do this, repeating these compassionate sentiments for four or five minutes, allowing the feelings involved in this act of compassion to grow as they will. Already we can note changes for the better as a result of our compassion meditation. Our compassion for the loved one grows, changing both us and them!

Here is a suggested prayer for your compassion meditation. Use it as you wish, change it to suit your own needs—but pray it as fervently as you can.

May you be happy
May you be free.
May you be loving.
May you be loved.
May the Lord bring you to the fullest completion that his love calls you.
May every fiber of your being resonate to the glory to which God calls you.
May you be successful in your every endeavor.
May you experience the fullness of peace in body and soul.
May you know the Lord in all his goodness.
May you forgive every transgression.
I forgive you with all my heart and soul.
May you know what it means to be a child of God.
May you experience the glory of possessing the kingdom of God.
May you live and walk in peace and fellowship with all of God's creatures.
May every blessing be yours.
May goodness and love show itself in everything that you do and in all that is done to you.
May you be one with all of God's creation.
May you experience the blessings of God's grace for all eternity!

In the second step we chose another person, an indifferent or neutral person. This should be someone whom we know of but whom we really don't know, a casual acquaintance, someone we saw in the news, the postman, the grocery clerk, a stranger on the bus, or the woman who sat next to us in the theater. Then we simply take the same compassionate emotion we experienced in the first steps and transfer it to this second person. That's right. We take this previous, intimate, personal, loving sentiment which we feel for our mother, father, friend, or child, and which probably has been gained only after years of self-giving and sacrifice and freely and willingly transfer it to a stranger. We wish this stranger (who can never really be a stranger any more, even if we never see him/her again) all of the same loving impulses and sentiments of joy, peace, happiness, healing, life, and contentment that we felt in the first step. We do this for about five minutes, returning as often as necessary to our awareness of the first step in order to recapture our authentic feeling of compassion in order to transfer it. Another wonderful change is being wrought. Neither we, nor this stranger can ever be the same as we were before.

In some ways I have found this second step even more difficult than the third, which is to choose an enemy for compassion. We are used at least to the idea of loving our enemies. As for loving those who love us, we are told even pagans do this. But what about the neutral person, the stranger, the mass of humanity. Here, at least, is a beginning, where we select a neutral individual and lavish upon him/her freely and without any ulterior motive all that personal and sacred love we have stirred up from step one. The difficulty stems, no doubt, from this lack of ulterior motive. Love must be freely given for its own sake. Indeed, love only begins when nothing is expected in return. Paradoxically it can be a wonderfully freeing experience to lavish our compassion on an unknown and undemanding stranger.

The third step is to choose an enemy. For some this may, at first, be difficult. Exactly who is our enemy? We may not be aware of anyone whom we actually hate or who hates us. Yet the surprising thing here turns out to be how many enemies we do have. An enemy can be someone we oppose or who opposes us. It can be a public person, one with ideological differences, an unknown (e.g., an ecologically destructive person) or even a collective (e.g., the neo-Nazi Party). Our enemy, like our beloved in step one, may also be someone from our past, living or dead, for whom forgiveness is still possible and overdue.

Once again we contact the compassion we felt in step one and deliberately transfer these feelings to our enemy. We go back as often as necessary to get in touch our loving emotions as we wish peace, joy, benignity, kindness, gentleness, patience, and all the fruits of the Spirit (Gal 5:22). We must possess these ourselves to some degree, in order to share them, but in the very process of this compassion meditation we are graced with these fruits. We are reaching into the very ground of our true selves, the center of our own Christ-consciousness and trapping an infinite reservoir of compassion-to-be shared.

Our own compassion grows with the sharing. Compassion meditation is an art and perfects itself with practice. It reacts directly against our massive false-self system revealing it for what it is. It opposes the illusory world view into which we are thrown from birth (original sin) and frees us to choose authentically as beings in touch with, and in harmony with, our true selves.

Obviously compassion meditation is not the solution to all of our problems, but it is a significant step forward. It does make an authentic grasp through the obscurities, illusions, and self-deceptions which hinder our progress toward wholeness, Christ-consciousness, and forgiveness.

26
Centering Meditation

Officially, at least, the monks of my community are contemplatives. We are said to belong to a contemplative order, but what does that mean? Part of the answer may be seen any morning in our darkened church from 4:00 to 5:00 A.M. The still figures of the white-clad monks can barely be made out scattered here and there throughout the church. Some are sitting on cushions on the floor, others, more traditionally, in the choir seats. Until the clock in the cloister chimes the half-hour, there is not a stir. But then the monks arise and begin a silent, ten-minute walking meditation, covering the full circuit of the church, until they once again reach their original seats. Again they take their preferred positions and resume their meditations.

But is this contemplation? Are the monks engaged in contemplative prayer? There is no way to answer that question on an individual basis except by asking each individual monk. Certainly they are taught the principles of contemplative prayer, and there is a certain presumption even before they entered the monastery that deep prayer was a part of their lives.

Perhaps there are better words to describe the monks or the monastic lifestyle. Some prefer *a contemplative attitude* to *contemplation*. This extends contemplation from something done merely at assigned prayer-times to an attitude of listening to God that extends throughout the day. Still others feel that "a monastic lifestyle" is sufficient. At any rate, contemplative prayer is sometimes easier to experience than to describe.

In the First Book of Kings, chapters 18 and 19, we read the fascinating account of the prophet Elijah and Queen Jezebel. Jezebel was the wife of Ahab, who had married her in spite of the prohibition forbidding Jews to marry Philistines. To make matters worse, when Jezebel came to assume the throne of Israel, she brought with her four hundred and fifty prophets of Baal and four hundred priests of the goddess Ashera.

Elijah was fed up with King Ahab's fence-sitting. "If Yahweh is God, serve him," he declared, "if Baal, then follow him." Then he told Ahab to summon all of Israel together with all of Jezebel's pagan priests and prophets to meet with him on Mt. Carmel. It was time for a showdown.

Elijah had two altars built and told the people to bring two bulls for sacrifice. The pagans were to prepare one bull and lay it on the wood without setting fire to it. Then they were to invoke Baal to cause a fire to consume their offering. Elijah would do likewise and call upon Yahweh. The one who answered by fire was to be recognized as God.

So from morning until noon the priests called upon Baal by name, "Baal, Baal, answer us." But there was no reply. They shouted louder and, as was their custom, danced with abandon around the altar. All afternoon they ranted and raved and gashed themselves with knives and spears until the hour of the evening sacrifice. Still there was no reply, no sound, no sign of awareness.

Elijah then prepared his bull, laid it upon the wood, and told the Jews to fill four jars with water and pour them over the animal and the wood. They did this three successive times, and the water ran over the altar and filled the trench Elijah had ordered to be dug around it. Then Elijah stepped forward and offered a simple prayer to Yahweh. Suddenly the fire of the Lord fell from out of the heavens and consumed the whole offering and the wood. It licked up the water in the trench and scorched the very stones of the altar and the earth on which it stood. When the people saw this, they fell on their faces and cried, "Yahweh is God, Yahweh is God." At this point, Elijah ordered the people to seize the prophets of Baal, take them down to the Kishon, and slaughter them there in the valley.

Ahab rushed to his wife Jezebel and told her all the Elijah had done and how he had put all of prophets to the sword. Enraged, Jezebel sent a messenger to Elijah. "May the gods curse me," she said, "if by this time tomorrow, I have not taken your life as you took theirs." Elijah was afraid and fled for his life. But his troubles had just begun. He got as far as Beersheba in Judea where he despaired and asked the Lord to take his life. Instead, the Lord sent an angel to give him bread and water. He ate and drank and, nourished by this food, went on for forty days and forty nights until he reached Horeb, the mountain of God (Horeb is another name for Mt. Sinai). Elijah entered a cave and waited.

He was told to go and stand on the mountain before God, who would pass by. Suddenly a great and strong wind came, rending the earth and shattering the very rocks before him. But the Lord was not in the wind. And after the wind there was an earthquake which made the mountain tremble and caused the stones to fall in an awesome landslide, but the Lord was not in the earthquake. And after the earthquake, fire, but the Lord was not in the fire. Then Elijah heard the sound of a gentle breeze, and when he heard it, he hid his face in his cloak and went out and stood at the mouth of his cave. Then a voice spoke to him.

Something very interesting is happening here. There is a deliberate contrast shown in the manner in which God spoke to Elijah and in the manner in which he had spoken to Moses and the people in the past. The author of the Book of Kings wants us to see Elijah in terms of the past, but with a difference.

During the time of their sojourn in the desert, the Jews had been a crass, ignorant people who could only be brought to God by fear and a display of his power. When the Lord promised to speak to them (Exodus 20), Moses was told to put barriers around the mountain. Any man or beast who so much as touched the edge of the mountain was to be stoned. And there were peals of thunder and flashes of lightening, dense clouds, and a loud blast of trumpets. The people waiting there at the foot of the mountain were terrified. The sound of the trumpets grew ever louder, and whenever Moses spoke, the Lord answered him in peals of thunder.

Note the similarities between the story of Moses and story of Elijah. Moses and the people were fleeing persecution from a pagan ruler. Elijah was fleeing persecution from Jezebel. Moses wandered in the desert for forty years. Elijah wandered in the desert for forty days and forty nights. Moses and the people were fed by a miracle from God. Elijah was given food and drink by an angel. Both were told to go to Mt. Sinai where God would meet and speak to them. But here the similarities end.

The contrast now is quite deliberate and is repeated in three different ways. God will no longer speak to his people through fear. He is explicitly said not to have been in the wind, the earthquake, or the fire. Rather now he is recognized in quiet, in the peaceful sound of a gentle breeze.

We can take this story one step further, to another mountain at another time. On Mt. Tabor we have the same cast. There were Elijah and Moses talking to Jesus. And suddenly there was a cloud and from the cloud the voice of God spoke. His command was a step further even than hearing him in the silence of Elijah. His command now is to accept Jesus as his beloved son and listen to him.

This is contemplative prayer, listening to God. Not only listening to God but also hearing him, and especially hearing him in silence, beyond words, and without images. This is the task of contemplative prayer.

There are many reasons for the decline in both the interest and the practice of contemplative prayer in our culture. Until recently, the United States was a frontier nation with little of the leisure time necessary for contemplation. The so-called Protestant ethic, which held that God rewards the hard-working with material prosperity, and the fact that the Church in America has been missionary-oriented and activistic, tended to minimize the attraction to contemplative prayer.

On the other hand, contrary factors have led to a reaction against the materialistic, superficial level of consciousness that has dominated Western culture, and hence necessarily the Church, in the West. Many people, especially the young, have questioned the super-materialism of the American consumer society. Not having had to engage in their parents' struggle for security and financial success, they are able to look critically at some of the values which have overemphasized this success. And so, many of America's younger generations have begun to search for a deeper meaning for living and a deeper level of consciousness such as that involved in contemplative prayer. (Obviously this search is not limited to the young).

Answers, sometimes partial ones, sometimes wholly mistaken ones, have been sought and found, for example, in Eastern types of meditation, esoteric cults, even in drugs and alcohol. Forms of meditation, some of them authentic, some not so authentic, abound in our youth cultures. Gurus, Zen sitting, Yoga,, TM have outlasted the 1970s, and all of them attempt to teach meditation techniques. Sometimes these techniques are taught as prayer. At other times they are specifically presented as a merely natural activity performed for merely natural ends. Almost all of them involve a wordless, thought-transcending process that may closely resemble contemplative prayer and may even help one come closer to it. But I think it is important for us to realize that we need look no further than our own Church to find an authentic, well-proven, simple, and theologically sound approach to contemplative prayer.

As interest has been rekindled in the Church in general, contemplative prayer has leapt over the wall. No longer is it confined to convents of Poor Clares or Trappist monasteries.

It is returning to common practice within the Church. Books, articles, tapes, retreats, and workshops on centering prayer are becoming quite common. Abbot Butler, an expert on Western mysticism, refers to contemplative prayer as taught in *The Cloud of Unknowing* (a fourteenth-century treatise on contemplative prayer by an unknown English author) as a teachable form of contemplation. Not only, he says, is it apt for priests and religious, but for the man and woman in the street.

Many people, however, seek meditation techniques as ways of rushing into contemplative prayer without proper preliminaries. Although no given individual can be forced into the theoretical structure of prayer as taught by the spiritual masters of the Western (Christian) tradition, there is a generally valid and universally experienced process of stages of growth from lower forms of prayer to higher. Most of us, in some way or other, have to go through these growth stages.

The great master of contemplative prayer, the author of *The Cloud of Unknowing*, warns against a too-hasty or too-superficial interest in the higher forms of prayer:

> I charge you with love's authority, if you give this book to someone else, warn them (as I warn you) to take the time to read it thoroughly.... I fear lest a person read only some parts and quickly fall into error. To avoid a blunder like this, I beg you and anyone else reading this book, for love's sake to do as I ask.

> As for worldly gossips, flatterers, the scrupulous, talebearers, busybodies, and the hypercritical, I would just as soon they never laid eyes on this book. I had no intention of writing for them and prefer that they do not meddle with it. This applies also to the merely curious, educated or not. They may be good people by the standard of the active life, but this book is not suited to their needs.[4]

---

[4]   William Johnston, ed. *The Cloud of Unknowing* (New York: Image Books, 1973), 43.

Then he goes on to describe those whom grace has prepared to grasp his message. These are people who, every now and then, taste something of contemplative love by way of the action of the Holy Spirit in the very center of their souls, exciting them to love. This ought to include every Christian, at some point in his or her life. That is to say, contemplative prayer, in some form or other, really is for everyone. Instead of speaking of the extraordinary grace of contemplative prayer (the beginnings of which, at least we are here equating with centering prayer), we should speak of the extraordinary grace of prayer itself. Given this great miracle, contemplative prayer, as well as every other degree or intensity of prayer, ought to follow.

In his commentary on the Our Father, Origen, one of the earliest theologians of the Church, says that the most marvelous thing about this prayer is not any particular phrase included in it but the very fact that we can say it at all. The extraordinary grace lies in our God-given ability to bridge the infinite gap between God and us and to converse with God face to face. Once we understand this, the place which contemplative prayer can and should have in our spiritual lives is no longer a problem.

Prayer differs from prayer, not in essence, but merely in its degree of intensity. Basically, the simplest recitation of the Our Father in faith, hope, and love by any child is the same as the most profound communion with God of the greatest mystic in a silence beyond words. The difference can be found in degree or intensity, but not in the nature of prayer itself.

In any prayer, of whatever type or intensity, the one praying so enters into the triune life of God as to become one with the Holy Spirit as the fullest expression of the love of the Father for the Son and of the Son for the Father. He becomes, as it were, Holy Spirit; the prayer activity becomes the Trinitarian expression of God loving himself.

How do we begin to practice contemplative prayer? *The Cloud of Unknowing* tells us. First, we have to know and love

God. This means we should already have developed a basic prayer life that is much more than a simple asking for favors. And as *The Cloud of Unknowing* says in chapter 35, "If you seek contemplation you must cultivate study and reflection in prayer." Frequent meditative reading of the Scriptures, good spiritual reading habits, and the frequent practice of traditional meditation would answer this requirement. We would include here also, reception of the sacraments. As *The Cloud* says in chapter 28,

> When should someone begin the contemplative work? Only when he has first cleansed his conscience of all particular sins in the sacrament of penance as prescribed by the Church. After confession, the source from which evil springs will still remain in his heart despite all his efforts, but eventually the work of love will heal them. And so a person should first cleanse his conscience in confession and, once having done this, he should without fear begin the work of contemplation (p. 85).

From these practices one is usually led to what *The Cloud* calls a stirring of love, a simple, peaceful inner desire to love God in and for himself with no other motivation. When we experience this stirring, we are already on the threshold of contemplative prayer. Many, many people know this experience, but would hesitate to think of themselves as contemplatives. The reason for this has already been mentioned. We have been accustomed to feel that this type of prayer is reserved for a few chosen souls, perhaps only for members of cloistered orders.

True enough, it is reserved for chosen souls, but not for merely a few, because we are, all of us, chosen souls. Once we have an experience of this stirring of love, all we need are a few simple instructions to enable us to begin contemplative prayer. The author of *The Cloud of Unknowing* says that there are people presently engaged in the active life who are being prepared by grace to grasp the message of his book. He is thinking of those who feel the mysterious activity of the Spirit in their inmost being, moving them to love. He does not say that they continually feel this stirring, as experienced contemplatives might, but every now and then, they taste something of contemplative love in the very heart of their being.

The instructions as found in the The Cloud of Unknowing can be given in four very simple rules. The first rule he gives is: Sit easily. We should be comfortable, so kneeling is not (as a general rule) the best position for disposing ourselves for contemplative prayer. We should be in a quiet place, of course, in a comfortable position, away from doorbells and telephones.

The second rule is: Place yourselves in the presence of God by a simple, brief prayer in your own words. There is a popular Byzantine prayer given to me by a priest of that rite who only came to an understanding of its content when he learned meditation, or contemplative prayer, as found in The Cloud:

> Serene light, shining in the ground of my being, draw me to yourself. Draw me past the snares of the senses, out of the mazes of the mind. Free me from symbols, from words, that I may discover the signified, the word unspoken in the darkness that veils the ground of my being.

It is sufficient, of course, for one to make a prayer in his own words, placing before God what he is about to do.

The third rule is simply: Love God. This is both difficult and easy. In a very real sense, if we had gotten as far as the third rule we are already engaged in loving God, and this is what contemplative prayer is all about. At this point, however, we don't try to think about God. We don't meditate on his attributes, or ask him for favors, or call to mind theological doctrine:

> At certain times and in certain circumstances it may be helpful to dwell on some particular situation or activity; during this work it is almost useless! Thinking and remembering are forms of spiritual understanding in which the eye of the spirit is opened and closed upon things somewhat as the eye of the marksman is on his

target. But during this work of love, everything you dwell on becomes an obstacle to union with God. For there is no room for him if your mind is cluttered with these concerns (chap. 5, p. 53).

And with all due reverence, he goes so far as to say that is useless to think we can nourish our contemplation by considering God's attributes, his kindness or his majesty, or by thinking about Our Lady, the angels, the saints, or about the joys of heaven, marvelous as these are. This activity, he says, is no longer of any use to you.

Of course, it is laudable to reflect on God's kindness and to love and praise him for it. Yet it is far better to let your mind rest peacefully in the awareness of him in his naked existence and to praise and love him for what he is in himself. Perhaps the best thing we could do is simply call upon God with love, and this in the fewest possible worlds. In chapter 37, the author of *The Cloud* says that contemplatives seldom pray in words, and if they do, their words are few. A word of one syllable is more suited to the spiritual nature of this work than longer words. The word Christ himself used might be best for this: Abba, Father, or, as *The Cloud* suggests, simply the one-syllable word, God. So we simply, peacefully place ourselves in Gods' presence and allow the love we have for him to express itself quietly in our hearts. We need do nothing else. This is contemplative prayer.

> This is what you do. Lift your heart up to the Lord with a peaceful stirring of love, desiring him for his own sake, and not for what he might give you!. Focus all your attention and desire on him and let this be the only concern of your mind and heart. Do all you can to forget everything else, holding your thoughts and desires free from involvement with any of God's creatures, either in general or in particular (chap. 3, p. 48).

Now it is true that we love God in serving others, but we should likewise love God in himself immediately and personally, and this is what we do in contemplative prayer.

If you find that this approach to contemplative prayer appeals to you (and keep in mind that there are many different approaches), then you should try it. You should try it daily, even twice daily, for fifteen or twenty minutes each time. Allow God to draw you to himself even to the point where you find that you have, without knowing it, ceased to speak in your heart the words "Abba, Father," but have been lifted above symbols and words into the quiet stillness of God's presence in the very center of your being.

The fourth and final rule is: End your period of contemplation with a simple vocal prayer such as the Our Father, said very slowly and carefully. Take a full two or three minutes. This will help to bring you back to everyday consciousness. This is necessary because contemplation does tend to lift us out of ourselves.

Falling asleep in the context of contemplative prayer need not be a problem. If you fall asleep during this work of love of God, you should thank God. Sleep must have been needed at that time, and God gave it as a gift. We simply return to our prayer "Abba, Father," when we realize that we may have nodded off or given in to distraction.

In regard to distractions, *The Cloud* advises us that:

> . . . when distracting thoughts come, you should pretend that you do not even notice their presence or that they have come between you and your God. Look beyond them— look over their shoulder, as if you were looking for something else, and of course you are. For surely beyond them God is hidden in the dark cloud of unknowing. Do this, and you will soon be relieved of anxiety (chap 32, p. 88).

A bit later he goes on to tell us that there is another strategy we are welcome to try. When you feel utterly exhausted from fighting your thoughts, you say to yourself, "It's futile to fight with them any longer." Then lie down before them like a captive or a coward. When you do, you commend yourself to God in the midst of your enemies, and you admit the radical weakness of your nature. He suggests that you remember this device particularly, for in employing it, you place yourself completely in God's hands.

If you would like to know if this type of prayer is for you, let me conclude with the words of *The Cloud of Unknowing*, chapter 75, which discusses certain signs by which one can determine whether or not God is drawing him to contemplation. The author of *The Cloud* says:

> Let a man examine himself to see if he has done everything he can to purify his conscience of deliberate sin according to the precepts of the Church and the advice of his spiritual director. Once he is satisfied on this account, all is well but to be even more certain, see if he is habitually more attracted to the simple contemplative prayer than to any other spiritual devotion. And then, if his conscience leaves him no peace in any exterior or interior work he does, unless he makes this secret little love based upon the The Cloud of Unknowing his principal concern, it is a sign that God is calling him to this prayer (p. 145).

And finally, remember this admonition: If you wish to continue growing, you must nourish in your heart the lively longing for God. Though this loving desire is certainly God's gift, it is up to you to nourish it.

27
The Process of Focusing

Focusing was developed by Dr. Eugene Gendlin of the University of Chicago in the early 1960s (see bibliography). He insists that he did not discover the process but rather uncovered it. It is something that belongs to the human race. We spoke in chapter 14 about the three centers of human knowledge. There is the brain center (the scarecrow), which is the most commonly accepted way of knowing in our society. Then there is the heart center (the tin man), also an easily accepted way of knowing. The third center, the body or the guts (the lion), is not so well known or accepted. The body, however, is an agent of knowing for us as well as the brain and the heart. Focusing is concerned with using our body knowledge to bring us to healing. The body knows what its wholeness is. Look at how it heals a physical wound. It first speaks to us of its hurt by way of pain. Then it proceeds to heal the hurt in ways that modern science knows almost nothing about. The final healing, even though it leaves a scar, leaves the tissue even stronger than it was before the wound was inflicted. If the body knows that it was hurt, and knows how to heal a hurt, then it also knows what its wholeness is

When we speak of the body, we actually are speaking of the whole person because even our brains and our hearts are part of the body. Thus our body hurts are not merely what we call physical wounds but can be any wounding we receive on any level including spiritual, psychological, or emotional. When we receive such a wound, the body alerts us by sending us a signal, pain. The source of some forms of pain are easily recognizable, such as the pain from a cut or a ruptured appendix. Other kinds of "pain," such as headaches, anxiety, butterflies in the stomach, depression, or sadness, are strongly felt, but we frequently don't know what caused them. Thus the body keeps sending these signals to alert us to deal with a wound we don't even recognize. The body usually keeps sending a pain signal until we pay attention to it and deal with the wound, whatever kind it may be. Sometimes this "pain signal" goes on for many years.

For wounds that are interior, or as we say, mental, the body alerts us just as it does for physical wounds. The body is willing to inform us (body knowledge) what that pain is about and is willing and able to lead us to wholeness and a cessation of all pain. We have to listen to what the body is telling us.

This listening to body knowledge is an ability that has been lost in modern civilization. It involves an embracing of pain so that we can hear what it is saying. In our culture the response to pain is a running away. Just as a child defines hole as "something to dig," we today define pain as "something to get away from." We have all kinds of ways to do this: medicine, drugs, alcohol, sex, work.

Focusing is the process that enables us to hear what the body is telling us, through feelings, about our wounds and what to do about them. It can be used for other things involving body knowledge, such as dreams or spiritual insights in prayer or Scripture reading, but, for our purposes here, we will limit it to the healing of wounds.

Here is a simple explanation of the focusing process. You can actually experience it as you go through the instructions:

1. Sit quietly for a moment; take several deep, slow breaths. Offer this prayer, or a similar one in your own words:

Dear Lord, thank you for gracing me to spend these few moments in your presence. I would like to respond to the innate ability you give me to listen to my body's knowledge. I want to recognize that pain is my body's way of calling my attention to my hurts and that it is also a means to lead me into the healing process. You have never promised me, as a Christian, that I would be free from pain (crosses). But you have promised to be with me in my trials and sufferings and to bring me through them to a new and grace-filled life. Amen.

2. Now feel your body. Perhaps you might give your attention to your solar plexus (guts!), the location of many vague, uncomfortable feelings. Indeed, some people are constantly affected by unfocused, abiding discomfort here. They have never known what these feelings mean or how to deal with them. Go through your whole body—are there any puzzling pains, aches, feelings, anywhere that you cannot account for? Simply let them arise. Don't do anything for a while but just feel! Give your body three or four minutes to speak to you through some feeling or other. Body knowledge takes longer than intellectual knowledge. Don't be concerned with the first thing that *comes to mind* but wait for something to come to your body feelings. It may be connected to what is in the mind or it may not. Just allow the feeling to be there. Do not do anything else. The feeling may be a physical (e.g., muscle) pain, it may be excitement, fear, heaviness, or depression. What ever it is, it is the body speaking. Don't run from it. This is what we do too often. Drugs, alcohol, medicine, sex, and work are the ways we use to get away from body knowledge. Today, you are not going to run. You are going to listen—even though it hurts. If it is very painful just reach out in your heart to God who is present to

you and who will accompany you in your search for healing. Allow yourself to weep if this is called for. Weeping is also body language. Realize that whatever you feel is a call for healing. It is not an enemy but a friend and a teacher. Just accept it and be with it for a little while.

3.   Now let this vague feeling speak to you. It will do so, not intellectually, but by way of your imagination, by images and by a new feeling. Something will come to your mind (imagination). It may be a mental picture, a color, a song, a word, a scenario from your past life, a dream, or whatever. Do not control it but just let it happen. It may take a few seconds or a few minutes. You will not realize it is *coming*. It will suddenly just *be there*. Do not look for anything. Let your body knowledge (not your brain) give you what it wants. Do not look for symbols as intellectually decipherable signs that make sense. Do not try to make sense of what comes. Your brain may try to interfere and to "interpret" what comes; just ignore it.

4.   As something comes, and something will, accept it. Now relate whatever comes to the feeling you experienced in step 2. You will notice a difference, slight or strong, in what you feel. It may be heavier, lighter, in a different part of the body, more expansive, darker, releasing. This is an important step in the body-knowledge process. Don't try to "make sense" of it. Just let it happen and be aware of it.

5.   Next, just be with this new thing (image) and its new feeling. Don't analyze or interpret it. Just accept it. If it is painful, remember that it is not an enemy but a friend and teacher. Just go with it—appreciate it. Now allow something else to come, a new image, picture, sound, color, feeling, or word. It may take a few minutes or only a few seconds. Beware of any

intellectualizations. The brain will want to step in and halt the process. It does not know how to deal with body knowledge and wants to substitute thoughts for feelings. If thoughts could heal, you would never have these feelings. Don't look for a logical connection with your new image and/or feeling. Logic is brain work. Just wait for something to come. If nothing comes, say to yourself: "O.K., body, give me a step forward in this. Speak to me." Then when something comes, accept it and its accompanying new feeling. It will feel a bit (or a lot) different from your last image and feeling. Just let it be there and appreciate it.

6. Repeat this process with the new image and feeling. Each time you do this, you will be a further step forward in the healing process. You may do it only one or two times or a dozen times. At some point you will notice that you no longer feel so bad or in pain. The feeling accompanying an image will be expansive, light, no longer problematic. It will be good, wonderful, or at the very least O.K.

7. When this kind of feeling comes, accept it. Notice, by contrast, how you feel now with how you felt when you began the focusing process. You have gone from a vague, discomforting or even painful feeling to a good one. This is your body leading you forward in the healing process. You will discover that the issue you began with is not as bad as it was—maybe it is no longer even an issue. If you think you are at this point, ask your body: "Body, is it O.K. to stop here for now?" Your body will give you a clear answer—yes or no! If the answer is no, continue the process until the answer is yes.

8. You may use this focusing process for any feeling that comes up when you want to do step 1. You may have

many feelings to deal with from many wounds—or only a few. It is a thing you can do, all through your life, whenever you feel the need. It is a healing process always available to you.

9. Finish your focusing with an appreciation of what you now feel by contrast to how you felt when you began. This is a grace—a gift from God. Thank him for it.

The focusing process actually continues as you take up your daily routine. Thoughts (now using "brain knowledge") about the experience will show interconnections, symbolic interpretations, and further revelations from the focusing process. This process can be especially valuable for people who practice centering prayer. Sometimes in this wordless meditation, deep and painful issues can arise from the subconscious. If they are important issues (strongly felt), interrupt your meditation and focus on them. If they are not so important, "look over their shoulder" as the author of *The Cloud of Unknowing* advises, but focus on them after your meditation is over.

This same focusing process can be used in our Scripture meditation. When we read or listen to the Scriptures and a particular incident, parable, phrase, or even a single word "leaps out and grabs us" and brings with it a body feeling or sensation of anxiety, guilt, unfinished business, puzzlement, or even joy, we can use it to focus. It can also be used to allow the gut center (the lion) to teach us the meaning of dreams that leave us with a body feeling of some kind.

28

Vulnerability—
An Ounce of Prevention

When he came to his senses, he said, "How many of my father's hired men have food to spare, and here I am starving to death!. I will set out and go back to my father and say to him: Father, I have sinned against heaven and against you. I am no longer worthy to be called your son; make me like one of your hired men." So he got up and went to his father. But while he was still a long way off, his father saw him and was filled with compassion for him. (Lk 15:17–20).

This is truly a story of forgiveness, the Parable of the Prodigal Son. It is your story, my story, and God's story. When we "come to our senses," we will realize that there is no need to continue to afflict ourselves. We will humble our pride, which means simply to face who and where we are, begin the journey, the process of forgiveness, back to our Father's house.

Please notice that the Prodigal Son would not have been drawn back to his father's house when he finally came to his senses, unless he had some assurance of forgiveness. He knew his father would forgive him because he knew, and no doubt had experienced many times before, that his father was *vulnerable.* The word means, "able to be wounded."

Vulnerability is one of the by-products of love. "[Love] is not easily angered, it keeps no record of wrongs "(1Co 13:5). God is vulnerable, and we are called to vulnerability. We are called to be the type of persons of whom someone knows that even if we have been hurt, they can turn to us and seek forgiveness. We will see them even "while they are a long way off" and be "filled with compassion."

An ounce of prevention in the forgiveness process will prompt us to be vulnerable. This does not mean that we can be stepped on with impunity again and again. It does mean that we are nonetheless willing to forgive our brother or sister "seventy times seven times." Many years ago. I was led by God's grace to make an interesting and helpful resolution. I remember hearing somebody say that most hurts are carried unwittingly and that often the perpetrators are unaware, both before and after the wound has been inflicted, that they have caused any harm. If then, I reasoned, someone does not have the intention of hurting me, but I am hurt just the same, who is responsible for my pain? No one but myself! Thus, I resolved never to allow myself to be hurt unless I was positive that the perpetrator deliberately and knowingly intended to hurt me. I have used this resolve dozens of times as an ounce of prevention. In ninety percent of the situations where someone has hurt me, I have not had to forgive them because there was nothing there to forgive. They did not *intend* to harm me.

Very often anger is one of the first reactions to being hurt. If we can deal with this anger right away and resolve it, we can apply the healing of the forgiveness process before it has a chance to cause anything deeper than a superficial wound. One way of dealing early with such anger is through a process which I call being free to love. I have already described this process as a way to deal with the anger stage (in chapter 12). I repeat some of it here as one of the useful tools in the wholeness process.

Jesus said, "But the things that come out of the mouth come from the heart, and these make a man 'unclean.' For out of the heart come evil thoughts, murder, adultery, sexual immorality, theft, false testimony, slander. These are what make a man 'unclean'"(Mt 15:18).As previously mentioned, some counselors think they we each have a vast reservoir of unspecified emotions. These are channeled to our internal world in such ways that our responses to our environment trigger them. When this emotional outpouring comes in the form of anger, it is a demanding, energetic, and consuming force. It is a defensive mechanism and, when uncontrolled, takes on an animal-like aspect. Its purpose is to forcefully intimidate another into doing something we want. Rarely is it compatible with forgiveness or love. Usually it consumes any energy we might have that could be channeled in the direction of these two desirable activities. Only when we are free from anger, can we be "Free to Love" (as in the cassette of that title in the bibliography).

Anger can be said to be triggered by any one or any combination of three desires. These are our desires for *security, control,* or *approval.* Just think of it for a moment. Recall an episode of your own anger or that of someone else. It is quite easy to recognize one or more of these desires behind it. I recall seeing a baby in a crib get so angry that his body trembled and his face turned scarlet. When his mother bent over to pick him up, he stopped crying, even before she touched him, as his whole body strained upward towards her. There was no longer any need for anger. His desire for control was satisfied. He instinctively manipulated his mother into picking him up. Indeed this is why crying is such an unpleasant sound. If we enjoyed hearing it, it would not be as manipulative.

Please note that I said that anger arises from the *desire* for approval, control, or security. This is not the same as approval, control, or security in themselves. It is the *desire* for one or another of them. Let me give you an example. One Sunday I was preaching in our monastery church. After I began, an infant in the front row started to cry. Her father seemed more amused than annoyed by the ruckus. I was annoyed. I had spent much time and energy in preparing my homily, and was well aware that the attention of the entire congregation was centered on the child. Briefly through my mind flashed several horror stories, told in the seminary, about priests who asked parents in similar situations to remove the child, only to have them leave the church—never to return! So this possibility was out of the question. But I could feel my anger rising, my face get red, and my annoyance showing itself in my voice inflections as I spoke.

In just one or two seconds I put myself through my free to love procedure. It can be done in a much briefer time than it can be described. My swift thoughts went like this: "That baby is crying and ruining my sermon. I am getting angry because of this, and my anger will be worse than the baby's noise. Why am I angry? Because I *desire* to control the baby. But I can't control her, and my animal defense mechanism triggered by her crying is totally ineffectual and could even be harmful. What can I do? If something is to be done, it must be done *within me*. I need to be free to love. It is true I cannot control the baby, but I can control my *desire* to control her." Do you see the difference? Control (or security or approval) is not in my power, but the *desire* to control is. All right then I willingly, freely, and deliberately surrendered my *desire* to control that baby. Almost immediately I felt my anger lessen. I was able to continue my sermon, even though I had to shorten it considerably, without chagrin but with patience and even affability. Also when the father apologized after Mass, I felt no need whatsoever to chide him or show annoyance. In fact, he congratulated me for my forbearance.

Do you understand the difference between control (approval, security) and the *desire* for control (approval, security)? To deal with our *desire* is always within our power. And it is the *desire*, not the control itself, that is responsible for anger.

This little free to love procedure is applicable in virtually all cases of anger. It must be remembered that you are not surrendering your principles or condoning the activity that brought about your anger. When a father discovers that his teenage son is going out on a Saturday night with a case of beer in his car, he becomes angry. He desires to control his son. He can vent the anger, turn the boy off, and maybe temporarily control the situation. But what if he says to himself: "I don't want my son to do this. I am angry and apt to do things that will interfere with my ability to love. I will give up my *desire* to control him. Then I will firmly and lovingly (but without irrational, animal anger) deal with the situation." Surrendering the *desire* to control (approve, secure) does not mean surrendering the *actual* control. It can mean securing it more effectively—but by love, not by anger (as I did with the baby's crying in church). The father with the teenager can then even manifest a deliberate, controlled anger if need be (as Jesus did with the money changers in the temple). It will then be motivated by love and not by an incoherent outrush of animal emotion. Anger can intimidate someone and even force an external change of behavior, but only love can really bring about effective change. We must be ourselves free to love.

Yet another ounce of prevention to anticipate the healing process before it is even needed is what I call the "Yes prayer." Whenever I recall a past incident that raises anger, annoyance, regret, or unforgiveness (and this seems to happen more often as I grow older), I deliberately call to mind that "Jesus is the eternal Amen to the Father." "Amen" means yes. So I pray: "Together with Jesus, I say yes to the past, yes to the present, and yes to the future. Amen to yesterday, amen to today, and amen to tomorrow." This is a practical way to accept God's will and to avoid hurts and their corresponding unforgiveness. Try it!

Another helpful ounce of prevention is to direct your anger to someone who will not be hurt by it. Strangely enough

I mean direct your anger to God. At one time in my life I would have thought that such an action would be blasphemous. Now I feel that it is really just a form of prayer. There are times of great traumas in all of our lives when we actually need to do this. What it actually is, is a cry for understanding. "Why do you, God, permit this suffering, death, illness, or tragedy?" We have a right to do this. Does not a loving parent permit a son or daughter such anger, arising as it does from pain or sorrow and its accompanying frustration and misunderstanding? The force of Jesus' cry on the cross is a perfect example. St. Matthew (27:46) says he cried out in a loud voice, "Why have you forsaken me?" Clearly this cry came from disillusionment, incomprehension, and anger. But it was at the same time a prayer. We are permitted to do likewise.

Vulnerability, then, is not only a product of the wholeness that results from the process of forgiveness; it is also a means to facilitate it and, even more importantly, a way to obviate the need for the process by preventing hurts from beginning.

Bibliography

Ashcroft, M. E. and H. B. Elliott *Bearing our Sorrows*. San Francisco: HarperSanFrancisco, 1993.

Bates, Lynda. *The Practice of Forgiveness*. Ogden, Utah: Copy Pro Printing, l993.

Bishop, Jr. and Mary Grunte, *How to Love Yourself When You Don't Know How*. Barrytown, N.Y.: Station Hill Press, 1992.

Campbell, P. and E. McMaho., *Bio-Spirituality (Focusing)*. Chicago: Loyola University Press, 1985.

Casarjian, Robin. *Forgiveness, Bold Choice for a Peaceful Heart*. New York: Bantam Books, 1992.

Desjardins, A. *Toward the Fullness of Life*. Putney, Vt.: Threshold Books, 1990.

Dossey, Larry. *Healing Words*. San Francisco: HarperSanFrancisco, 1993.

Flanigan, B. *Forgiving the Unforgiveable,* New York: Macmillan, 1992.

Kaufman, B. N. *Happiness Is a Choice*, New York: Fawcett Columbine, 1991.

Keyes, Ken, Jr. *Handbook to Higher Consciousness*. St. Mary, Ky.: Living Love Pub., 1975.

Linn, D. and M. *Healing of Memories*. New York: Paulist Press, 1974.

Meninger, William. *1012 Monastery Road,* Petersham, Mass: St. Bede's Pub., 1989.

———. *The Loving Search for God*, New York: Continuum, 1995.

———. *Free to Love, How to Deal with Anger.* Cassette tape, Snowmass Colo.: St. Benedict's Monastery, 1985

———. *Contemplative Prayer According to The Cloud of Unknowing.* Set of 4 cassette tapes. Snowmass Colo.: St. Benedict's Monastery, 1975.

———. *The Prodigal Son.* Cassette tape. Snowmass Colo.: St. Benedict's Monastery, 1980.

———. *The Process of Focusing and Contemplative Prayer.* Cassette tape. Snowmass Colo.: St. Benedict's Monastery, 1994.

Oliva, M., *Free to Pray, Free to Love,* Ave Maria Press: Notre Dame, Ind: Ave Maria Pres., 1994.

Simon, Sidney, and Suzanne Simon, *Forgiveness.* New York: Warner Books, 1990.

Partial Bibliography on the Enneagram

Hurley, Kathleen V., and Theodore E. Dobson. *What's My Type?,* San Francisco: HarperSanFrancisco, 1991.

———. *My Best Self.* San Francisco: 1993.

Keyes, M. F. *The Enneagram Relationship Workbook.* Muir Beach, Calif: Molysdatur Pub., 1992.

Metz, Barbara, and John Burchill. *The Enneagram and Prayer.* Denville, N.J.: Dimension Books, 1987.

Palmer, Helen, *The Enneagram.* San Francisco: Harper and Row, 1988.

———. *The Enneagram in Love and Work.* San Francisco: Harper SanFrancisco, 1995.

Riso, Don Richard. *Personality Types.* Boston: Houghton Mifflin Co., 1987.

———. *Understanding the Enneagram,* Boston: Houghton Mifflin Co., 1990.

———. *Enneagram Transformations.* Boston: Houghton Mifflin Co., 1990.

Rohr, Richard, and Andreas Ebert, *Discovering the Enneagram*. New York: Crossroad, 1990.

Zurcher, S. *Enneagram Spirituality*. Notre Dame, Ind: Ave Maria Press, 1992..